The Lip-Smacking Joys

. . . of America's favorite dessert are fully described and explored in this deliciously comprehensive book on the making, storing, freezing, and even the serving of Ice Cream.

Here are over 100 refreshingly original recipes, all using easily available natural ingredients, that make such treats as Apricot Almond Temptation and Watermelon Sherbet a possible taste rapture for everyone!

The fun of creating the luscious taste of homemade ice cream is now yours for the reading!

The Natural Foods Ice Cream Book

ROBERT O. SOMAN

PYRAMID BOOKS ▲ NEW YORK

THE NATURAL FOODS ICE CREAM BOOK

A PYRAMID BOOK

Pyramid edition published January, 1975

ISBN: 0-515-03575-0

Copyright © 1975 by Robert O. Soman

Library of Congress Catalog Card Number: 74–24437

Printed in the United States of America

Pyramid Books are published by Pyramid Communications, Inc. Its trademarks, consisting of the word "Pyramid" and the portrayal of a pyramid, are registered in the United States Patent Office.

PYRAMID COMMUNICATIONS, INC.
919 Third Avenue, New York, N.Y. 10022, U.S.A.

To the young at heart who want the pleasure of eating their own frozen natural desserts

Who Helped?

I have been involved with homemade ice cream for most of my life—as a child, turning the hand crank; as an adult, manufacturing the motor drive for an electric churn freezer, and always for pleasure at home.

When I started this book, I asked Angie Meyers, who was running a natural foods restaurant, to make and serve some of these ice creams. Students in an experimental food course at the Herbert H. Lehman College, where I was a guest lecturer, helped me with some comparison tests in natural recipes. In teaching them, I learned a lot. Many of our family's dinner guests and others commented and made suggestions. My wife, who is a professional writer and editor, gave me considerable assistance. But most of the credit goes to Frances K. Schoen, who is a member of the Greenhouse Association, New York's largest natural food cooperative. She had a hand in this book from the beginning to the end. She researched, she cooked, she typed, and she edited. Without her, much of the zest in this book would be missing.

In an overall sense, I, the author, represent a group, and therefore have used "we" throughout.

Contents

Part 1

How to Make Homemade Frozen Desserts

Come Along to Ice Cream Land

You or anyone in your family can create delicious homemade ice cream with old-fashioned farm-fresh taste. The best way to make it is with natural foods, the basis of all our recipes. The widest possible range of ingredients were used to illustrate how extraordinary frozen desserts can be. Some mixes require no cooking and are very simple to prepare; others give even the culinary expert new opportunities to invent gourmet treats. This book, in fact, is really a guide to many exciting adventures with your ice cream freezer. For purposes of general discussion, we have used the term "ice cream" in the broadest sense; it may also include "sherbets" or "ices."

A bucket churn freezer was used because of its versatility and popularity. At the present time, about one million of them are bought each year. With this cookbook, all freezer owners will be able to fully realize the many potentialities of their ice cream maker.

Ice cream can glamorize any part of your meal—or indeed of your day or night. Start dinner with a Cantaloupe Ice, use Cucumber Ice Cream on your favorite green salad, and finish your meal with Lemon Cheesecake topped with strawberries. For after-school snacks, give your children Peanut Butter Ice Cream. Tangerine Sherbet is an ideal thirst-quencher on a hot day. For late-night munching, take your favorite cottage cheese out of the refrigerator and turn it into the lightest, most satisfying nightcap in a few short minutes.

Special features of this book include helpful hints on preparing, freezing, and serving. Recipe comments also contain suggestions for flavor changes that can be easily adapted. You can start your ice cream career confident

13

of smashing success the very first time and never take a backward step. The flavor and satisfaction of custom-made frozen desserts that have been the province of emperors for centuries are now yours.

What Is Ice Cream?

Under a microscope, ice cream looks like a terrazo floor. There is a continuous pattern of ice crystals interconnected with unfrozen materials, surrounded by and interspersed with air cells.

The patterning comes about when ice cream is made. The mixture is placed in a freezer's container whose outside temperature is a few degrees below the freezing point of water. As the cold penetrates, the mix near the outside begins to stiffen. Little ice crystals begin to form in it, making the other ingredients more concentrated. Gradually, the entire mixture is thickened, as air is stirred in during the churning. Once the small, now heavier, particles and ice crystals are moved about, they tend to stay in place like marbles.

Federal standards for commercial ice cream and related products regulate such things as butterfat content and the amount of overrun (the amount of air whipped into ice cream). Many commercial ice creams are allowed to have a 100 percent overrun; in other words, the mix is doubled in volume by the powerful machines used. The finer commercial ice creams have less overrun. Homemade ice cream has 25 percent air, so it is thicker, richer, better ice cream.

In this book we have not been limited by sharp definitions but rather have included recipes created over the widest range of what are loosely called frozen desserts. However, we would like to give you some general definitions.

Ice cream is commonly used to denote frozen food made from a mixture of dairy products with a high percentage of butterfat, sweetener, and flavoring. It becomes smoother through whipping or stirring during the freezing process. (Otherwise, you would have a stiff frozen pudding.) Stabilizers, fruits, and nuts may or may not be added.

Stabilizers are optional ingredients in ice creams and other frozen desserts. Their main function is to help keep the texture of the ice cream from changing during storage. They aid in creating a smooth texture that is resistant to melting. Milk, cream, flour, eggs, and arrowroot are natural stabilizing materials. In some recipes in this book, gelatin is used as the stabilizing agent.

The two words *sherbet* and *ice* are often mistakenly used for the same mixture. There is a simple distinction between them. An ice is a frozen sweetened fruit juice or mashed or puréed fruit that is generally diluted with water and frozen in the same way as ice cream. A sherbet is similar to an ice except that milk or another dairy product is used in place of all or part of the water. Both products may be made with stabilizers.

Sherbets and ices are different from ice cream in that they generally have a higher sugar content, less air, and a coarser texture (because of more ice crystals and less butterfat). They also melt faster, which is why they feel cooler on the tongue.

What Goes Into Natural Ice Cream?

All the ingredients in your mixes should be of the best quality. Whenever possible, use natural, unrefined, unprocessed, and unsprayed foods. Only fresh ingredients will produce the full, rich-bodied flavor these frozen desserts should have.

You will find that, in addition to health food and specialty shops, many local supermarkets now stock natural foods, sometimes in special sections.

Here are brief descriptions of some of the foods we have used in preparing our natural frozen desserts. These foods are discussed because they are an important part of our recipes. A large variety of other natural products are available, and many regions have their own local specialties.

EGGS

Eggs often play an important part in the success of frozen desserts. Therefore, buy graded eggs in dated cartons. If they are available, you may find that fresh, fertile eggs, from hens that have been allowed to roam free, have a better taste.

The quantities produced by various recipes may vary slightly according to the freshness of the eggs and whether hand or electric beaters are used.

All eggs should be refrigerated promptly after purchase (the fertile ones are more perishable and have a shorter shelf life), because their flavor deteriorates at room temperature. As a general rule, eggs should be used as soon as possible—usually within a week.

Never use cracked or spoiled eggs; bacteria can get in and cause problems.

Don't throw away extra egg whites or yolks. Separated yolks will keep for days if you place them in a container with a tight cover, cover them with water, and refrigerate. The whites can be poured into individual ice cube trays and frozen until needed.

SALT

Sea salt or regular table salt may be used in any of these recipes. Sea salt, which is made from sun-evaporated seawater, is unrefined and is very rich in minerals of the sea.

Salt brings out the flavor and sweetness of the frozen mix, noticeably enhancing the flavor of ice creams made with eggs or nuts. In most ice creams the amount of salt added should be so small that its presence is difficult to detect. An overabundance of salt produces a sour taste and increases the time the mix takes to solidify.

HONEY

Honey is one of our best natural sources of sugar as well as a pure energy food that does not contain any artificial additives. All honeys are rich in minerals (such as copper, iron, magnesium, silica, chlorine, calcium, sodium, potassium, phosphorous), and contain small amounts of the vitamin B complex and some other trace substances. Always check honey labels for the key words "unheated" and "unfiltered." Natural vitamins can be destroyed in heating and removed by filtering.

When making frozen desserts avoid the darker types of honey such as buckwheat, which have strong flavors; the light and milder ones like clover, alfalfa, acacia, mesquite, sage, and clover (alone or in combinations) will not overpower the taste of the dessert itself but will simply act as a sweetener. Although tupelo looks very light, it has a very sweet taste, and you need less of it. If you and your family do not have a particular favorite, buy small quantities of the different varieties and experiment until you find the flavor that you like best.

Honey should be stored in a warm place, never below room temperature. After honey is opened, it should be refrigerated to keep it at its peak and free from mold. If crystals form, dissolve them by putting the container in warm water.

Honey used in place of sugar will cause frozen mixes to gel more slowly, and the final product will tend to be softer than those made with granular sugar.

Honey has a tendency to foam considerably when it is being heated. Therefore, when you use it in a mix, be careful that it does not boil over.

To measure honey accurately and easily, wet or lightly oil the cup or spoon first. Pour the honey out. Never dip the spoon into the honey container, because the added amount clinging to the spoon could make your mix too sweet or too liquid.

OTHER SWEETENERS

Based on your own taste preferences, you may find that occasionally you enjoy using some of the other natural sweeteners: blackstrap molasses, unsulfured molasses, date sugar, carob syrup, maple syrup, maple sugar, or sorghum.

Raw sugar or turbinado sugar is a granule form that has fewer nutrients than the natural sweeteners. It is also milder tasting in the final product and solidifies the mix more easily. It was used in certain recipes for both reasons. For instance, vanilla ice cream with honey as a sweetener would taste like honey ice cream, and we wanted to give you the pleasure of that lovely, clean vanilla.

Date sugar is a pure, natural sweetener made from pulverized and crystallized dates.

Maple syrup should be 100 percent pure syrup that has been produced without preservatives. Maple sugar is merely maple syrup that has been cooked until it granulates.

DRIED FRUITS

Use sun-dried fruits—apricots, currants, cherries, dates, figs, prunes, Monukka raisins (plump, black, seedless)—that are not sulfured or sugar-sweetened. These fruits are highly concentrated in natural sweetness.

Organically raised fruits keep best under refrigeration, especially during the summer. Their high natural sugar content gives them a long shelf life; however, they must be kept cool.

FRESH FRUITS

All fresh fruits should, if possible, be tree- or vine-ripened. If you are ripening them at home, place them in a cool, dark place, not in the sun. If you buy fruits that have been chemically treated, be sure to wash them well in warm water. Many people further advise that they be peeled if you suspect surface contamination.

To hasten the ripening of bananas, avocados, pears, and mangoes, place them in closed brown paper bags.

When certain fruits are not in season or cannot be found at your local markets, try using the natural fruit jams, as we have done for Guava Ice Cream.

SPICES AND FLAVORINGS

Use only pure vanilla extract or the vanilla bean itself. A 3-inch piece of the bean is equal to 1 tablespoon of extract. Pure vanilla brings out the natural sweetness and mellowness of fresh fruits.

Many natural food gourmets are finding carob to be a satisfactory replacement for cocoa and chocolate. Ounce for ounce, carob has a lighter flavor, and it is possible to keep increasing the carob content to the desired taste. The bitterness of chocolate makes it necessary to add a great amount of sweetener, whereas carob contains natural sugar.

Always buy small quantities of spices, as they lose their potency and flavor in storage. Since they do have a tendency to vary greatly in intensity and flavor, individual mixes should be tasted and adjusted to personal preference. Freezing decreases the strength of most flavorings, so flavorings should be used abundantly in frozen desserts.

When ice cream or mixes containing spices are not going to be eaten or frozen immediately after preparation, it may be necessary to reduce the amount specified because some spices tend to intensify the longer they stay in the mix.

Grated orange, lemon, and grapefruit rinds may be used interchangeably. You may find the flavor of the dried peels available at many fine spice shops to be stronger and want to adjust the amounts used accordingly.

Lemon juice enhances fruit flavors in frozen desserts and keeps many fruits from darkening, but it should be used sparingly.

For coffee flavoring, decaffeinated coffee should be used. It tastes about the same and will relieve any concern you may have about caffeine.

DAIRY PRODUCTS

Products such as goat's milk, goat's cream, nonfat dry powdered milk, soy milk, cow's milk and cream have been used in our recipes to provide the greatest possible variations. You will find that many of these dairy products can be substituted for one another.

Because the milk product often forms the greatest proportion of the mix, its taste can alter the flavor of the resulting product. Milk does not always have the same taste. It can be flavored by the foods eaten by the cow and it is also susceptible to absorption of strong odors. Therefore, all milk products should be tasted for sweetness and freshness. Fresh milk, cream, and milk products should always be refrigerated as soon as possible after purchase and should be kept tightly sealed.

The more cream used, the richer and smoother the ice cream will be. Cream also makes the mix whip rapidly, and produces a very satisfying flavor. The difference between light and heavy cream is the amount of milkfat; light cream contains between 18 percent and 30 percent, while heavy has 36 percent to 40 percent.

Half and half, a mixture of milk and cream containing at least 10 percent milkfat, can generally be substituted for light cream.

Goat's milk and cream were used in a few recipes. They are much more costly than cow's products. However, many people prefer them because they are easier to digest and are rich in nutrients and proteins. The actual taste of the ice cream is similar. Goat's milk is also sold in dried powder form.

Instant nonfat dry milk has had nearly all milkfat and water removed; however, it dissolves easily in water. After a package of nonfat dry milk powder is opened, it should be stored in a tightly sealed container, kept cool, and used within a month. A small percentage of moisture can double or triple the bacteria count. If dry milk is overexposed to the air, it may become lumpy and stale.

THE SOUR GROUP

Sour cream is light cream that has been subjected to a lactic acid culture to produce a creamy consistency and a tart flavor. (Milk or cream becomes sour when the milk's natural sugar, lactose, ferments to form lactic acid.) It usually contains between 18 percent and 20 percent milkfat.

Yogurt is a cultured milk product made by fermenting concentrated whole milk or partially skim milk enriched by the addition of nonfat dry milk with a combination of two different organisms to produce a tart, custardlike consistency.

Buttermilk is the liquid by-product when milk or cream is churned until the fat separates from it in the form of butter. It has a unique, tangy flavor. Most commercial buttermilk, however, is a cultured product made by treating pasteurized grade A whole milk, skim milk, partially skim milk, or reconstituted nonfat dry milk with a lactic acid culture. Butter granules are sometimes added.

Though they are produced by warming, all of the sour milk products must be kept tightly sealed and refrigerated so that the taste remains constant.

OTHER PRODUCTS

Soy, whole-wheat, and unbleached white flours as well as rice cream and millet were used in the recipes in this book. They are all delicious and full of nutritional value when used in their natural state.

Arrowroot, a natural thickening agent, has been used in some recipes rather than cornstarch, which is often treated with sulfur dioxide in processing.

Natural grains and seeds and nuts should be stored in a cool place; they must always be refrigerated in warm months. They should be kept in moisture-proof containers.

Wheat germ is a marvelous nutritional supplement and can be added to almost any mix without changing its flavor. Since it is highly perishable, it should be purchased in vacuum-packed tins and kept refrigerated after opening.

Apple juice may be substituted for apple cider. The latter can be a little stronger in taste but is not always available.

A WORD ABOUT ALL FOOD

Even if you do grow or make some of your own food, it is impossible to do it all by yourself. Therefore, be sure that the store you shop at and its products are reliable. Always read labels on containers and packages with a careful eye for any artificial additives or preservatives that you might not want to eat. Also, always check the last date of sale on dairy goods in order to get the freshest foods.

Above all, we wish you good luck and good (natural) frozen dessert eating. However, don't blame us if any of our recipes do not agree with you or if you like them too much and tend to overeat.

The tips given in this section will help making ice cream more delightful.

Line up everything you are going to use—including ice, rock salt, measuring spoons, and bowls—in the order of use; then read the recipe. It will give you a quick picture and may save that "oops, we forgot the . . ."

Put the cold ingredients back until you are ready for them. Leave the rest in line and push them back or put them away after use. If you are interrupted, you will know where you stopped.

TOOLS OF THE TRADE

A thin rubber spatula is most helpful for pushing down food that has spread over the sides of an electric blender, as well as for removing it.

A set of metal or strong plastic scoops are very helpful in handling the ice and salt.

A pair of cloth-lined rubber gloves with gauntlets will help you work with the ice.

Sponges should be on hand for wiping up spills and drippings.

A portable hand timer will be of immense value.

Most cooks wear a towel. For this type of job, we prefer a terry dish towel. Fold it like a paper airplane and attach the point to your apron, belt, or pants top.

If a recipe calls for hand-stirring during freezing or for transferring ice cream from one container to another, use a wooden spoon to prevent surface melting.

A flashlight will help you see the growing ice cream more clearly through a clear plastic lid.

THINK COLD AND CLEAN

Always keep bowls of hot and cold water handy, or work near a faucet, for the quick rinsing of utensils such as spoons, forks, measurers, and beaters, so that they are ready to use again immediately. But dip them in cold water before touching the mix again.

Incidentally, your chopping and slicing knife should be wet, for instance, to prevent crystallized ginger or other dried fruit from sticking to the knife when you chop or slice.

QUICKENING THE THICKENING

Gelatin must always be soaked in a little cold water for a few minutes in order to allow it to swell; it can then be dissolved by heating it over hot water or cooking it at a very low temperature. When very warm dissolved gelatin is stirred into a large amount of cold liquid, it may solidify. To avoid this, always stir an equal amount of cold liquid into the warm gelatin mixture, then stir the gelatin mixture into the remaining cold liquid.

Milk mixtures need constant stirring during cooking when being thickened with arrowroot, flour, or other stabilizers in order to prevent lumping. Thickening agents should always be combined with liquids first and cooked thoroughly before eggs are added.

SMOOTHER, BETTER CUSTARDS

When making custards, beat eggs with a wooden spoon; in this way only a little air is incorporated and a smoother custard results.

Careful temperature control is needed when eggs are used to thicken a custard mixture. Custards will always curdle if they are overcooked and if the temperature is too hot or uneven. To prevent this, always stir constantly, and use a double boiler when making custards. Should curdling occur, remove the pot from the heat and start beating the mixture vigorously.

If you want to cool your custard mixes quickly and don't mind a little additional work, place a saucepan containing the mixture in a large pan filled with ice cubes (or very cold water) and stir continuously with a wooden spoon until the mixture is thoroughly cool.

To prevent a skin from forming while the cooked custard mix is cooling, cover the surface with wax paper as soon as the pan is removed from the heat.

EGGS: CRACKING, SEPARATING, AND STIRRING

To separate an egg, crack the shell in the middle against the edge of a bowl. (If the shell is weak, tap the whole circumference of the egg with the edge of a sharp knife, rather than cracking it.) As the shell divides, let the white fall into the bowl and cradle the yolk in one half. Tip the yolk into the other shell half and let the white fall into the bowl. Put the yolk into another bowl.

Always combine beaten egg whites and other ingredients with a folding, not a stirring, motion. Mix thoroughly but only enough so that the ingredients are well blended.

Another caution against curdling: If you combine egg with a hot liquid or mixture of ingredients, always stir the liquid into the egg a little at a time or dilute the egg with a small amount of hot mixture and stir it into the remaining hot mixture. If it curdles, beat it.

NUTS: CHOPPING THE EASY WAY

If chopped nuts or dried fruits are to be added at the beginning of the freezing process rather than to the partially frozen ice cream after it has been churned and the dasher removed, then they must be cut very fine or they tend to clog the holes in the stirrer. This will decrease the amount of air in the final product.

Shelled nuts are more costly than nuts in the shell and don't keep as well.

Nuts may be chopped in several ways.

1. Place nuts on a chopping board and use a sharp-pointed knife. Keeping the point of the knife down, move the handle and blade up and down and work right to left across the board. Confine chopping action to the center of the board.

2. Place nuts between sheets of wax paper. Roll over the paper with a rolling pin, or press with your fingers.

3. Some blenders have a special setting for grinding nuts. Even if not, blenders are a fast way. Drop in a small quantity and cover. Set your blender at the highest speed for just a few seconds. Take the nuts out and add the next batch.

FRUITS: JUICES, RINDS, AND STORING

In order to get more juice from your lemons, leave them at room temperature for at least half an hour before squeezing and roll them over a hard surface with your hand first.

Lemon juice enhances fruit flavors in frozen desserts and keeps many fruits from darkening, but it should be used sparingly. Also, fruits should always be cut just before using.

Orange, lemon, lime, or grapefruit rinds can be grated and refrigerated in tightly covered containers. They keep a long time and are ready instantly for use.

A special word about fruit: When using fruit in any frozen desserts that are going to be stored in the freezer for any period of time, you must cut the fruit as small as possible or purée it as fine as possible to avoid the formation of large ice crystals on the pieces. Sweetened fruit tends to stay softer in frozen desserts.

MILK AND CREAM: COOKING AND WHIPPING

Before scalding milk and cream, rinse the saucepan in water. This helps to prevent a milk film from sticking to it.

Even though milk can be heated satisfactorily over direct heat, a double boiler usually works best because you can prevent overheating.

When whipping cream, chill the bowl and the beater as well as the cream for best results. Try to remember to put the bowl and beater in the refrigerator with the cream.

In homemade churn-type ice cream, heavy cream should be only lightly whipped prior to freezing because overwhipping results in a buttery texture that defeats the action of the churn freezer. For this reason, it is much safer to use a hand wire whisk rather than an electric beater for whipping.

Your Freezer

There are three ways to make frozen desserts at home. The oldest method is churn-freezing in a bucket. The classic churn freezer consists of a wooden or plastic tub, inside which is a covered metal can (sometimes called a canister). The ice cream mixture is poured into the can, where it becomes a frozen dessert. The space between the can and the inner wall of the tub is packed with ice and salt which combine to lower the temperature of the mixture and cause it to freeze. Inside the can, a scraper-aerator, known as a dasher, adds air and churns the mixture while it is freezing. The can, the dasher, or both revolve during the freezing process, turned either by hand cranking or by an electric motor.

Recently, a number of companies have developed a motorized refrigerator ice cream machine that works on the principle of the churn freezer except that ice and salt are not required. Mixtures are cooled by frozen air. The machine is placed in the freezer of the refrigerator or a deep freeze, and the electric cord is squeezed between the rubber seals on the freezer door and plugged into an outlet.

Last, there is still-freezing, also done in the freezing section of the refrigerator, but without the aid of any special ice cream unit. An ice cube tray or pan is filled with the mixture and placed in the freezer. While hardening, it may be removed from the freezer from time to time so that some air can be beaten in.

The comments that follow are based on years of experience with churn freezers. This experience is passed along to you in this book almost as a heritage.

CHURN FREEZERS

Bucket-type churn freezers have been available in the past in a wide range of sizes, from 1 pint to 25 quarts. The most common ones today are the 4- and 6-quart units. A 2-quart model with approximately 1 quart of mix was used in this book to make proportioning easier. Buy the size freezer that fits your average needs. On the occasions when you need larger quantities, you can make two batches of the same mix. Or you may want to try two different flavors for mix-and-match fun.

Freezers with a tall can appear to have a speedier churning action but are less convenient to handle than a shorter can. If the can has a clear plastic lid, you can watch the ice cream developing.

The wooden buckets provide excellent insulation and look homey but may leak unless soaked in water for several hours before use. The plastic models are satisfactory and come in attractive colors. Those with thick walls provide good insulation, but extra ice can make up for thinner walls.

Metal dashers with loose wooden sides give the best scraping action. Plastic dashers are usually designed for good scraping and superior churning. Either one will do a satisfactory job.

The hand-cranking models have been around for about 100 years. Many people think this is the only *real* way to make ice cream. A crew of youngsters usually enjoys taking turns at the handle. Because the hand models do not use electricity, they can be taken anywhere—on picnics, for example. For a few dollars more, the motor-driven freezer with its automatic churning has found its place along with other electrical labor-saving devices. Many people prefer this convenient way to make ice cream.

Assembling the freezer is very easy. Instructions (and a few recipes) prepared by the manufacturers accompany each unit.

In case you have misplaced the original booklet, we have made up a general set of our own instructions that are easy to follow. (See page 00.)

Getting Ready to Freeze

Making ice cream can be a fun activity for one person or a group. Some people enjoy cooking and working with recipes; others prefer operating a freezer and creating the final product; children like all the steps. Or you may want to do it all by yourself and take full credit.

MIXES

Get the mix you select ready for freezing. The mixes should always be as cool as possible. Starting the freezer with a warm mix increases churning time and consequently may cause a buttery texture. For best results, refrigerate the mix in a heavy plastic container for at least two hours before freezing; overnight is even better. However, if the mix contains gelatin as a stabilizer you cannot store it overnight because it will gel; such mixes should not be chilled for more than an hour. All mixes should be stirred thoroughly with a wooden spoon before being put into the freezing can.

THE FREEZER

Always check your freezer to see that all parts are in working order. If it is new or has not been used for a while, assemble it and make a three-turn dry run. Many dashers are made of one piece, usually plastic, but some of them—particularly the metal ones—have a separate scraper attached with loose screws to the metal. These screws should be left loose so they can automatically adjust to the inside of the can.

If you place a pan—one of the large plastic dishpans will do nicely—under your freezer, it will serve as a catchall while the freezer is in operation. It should be several inches wider than the bottom of your freezer tub. If too much water accumulates while the freezer is churning, the pan should be emptied.

Inspect and wash the canister, cover, and dasher thoroughly in hot soapy water. Rinse well in cold water and store in the refrigerator. Check the inside of the can carefully to remove any rust that may have formed. Place the cork from the cover in a safe place; you will need it later.

ICE

Get the ice ready. Approximately 10 pounds of ice in small sizes is needed for a 2-quart freezer (20 pounds for the 4-quart, 25 pounds for the 6-quart). This should provide a little extra ice. It is better to have more than less. If you prepare more than one batch, the ice remaining from the first can be reused, but you will need to add some fresh ice.

If you are not measuring the ice by the pound, a rough guide is that the freezing process will require approximately as much ice as will fill the bucket without the can. Hardening will take about half again as much.

You can start with ice cubes instead of cracked ice. Crush the cubes in a cloth or burlap bag with a mallet. Large pieces of ice will be unsatisfactory, as they can wedge between the sides of the bucket and the can. All snow, on the other hand, will melt quickly, but it has been used.

There are plastic chip ice trays on the market that produce instant crushed ice. However, you will need quite a number of them to fill a bucket.

Some people like to use large blocks of ice rather than ice cubes. They freeze water in empty cardboard milk containers or cooking pans, then chip these blocks with an ice pick.

For those late-night snacks or last-minute company-coming inspirations, you will want to have ice on hand. Therefore, anytime you're making ice cream at a leisurely rate, order or prepare enough extra ice for the next time. In your freezer, store what is not used in individual heavy-duty household plastic bags with small twist sealers on the tops.

When ice is stored, some of the pieces may stick together. The old-fashioned ice pick or a screwdriver will quickly break them into more manageable chunks.

SALT

Rock salt is usually available in the winter, so it is best to stock a supply then for summer use. The salt should always be kept in a dry place. If the salt crystals get congealed, an ice pick or screwdriver is very convenient for breaking them up.

Have the salt ready. It is a more critical element than the ice, so measure out the required amount carefully. (The 2-quart freezer needs 1 cup of salt, the 4-quart 2 cups, and the 6-quart 3 cups. Increase these amounts slightly when making sherbets and ices.) You may want to use three separate containers. Empty cans as well as paper or plastic cups are good for this purpose. Rock salt is preferable; however, fine table salt may be substituted. Just decrease the amount by $1/3$.

1. Put the dasher into the can; it will locate itself.

2. Pour the mixture into the can, leaving a minimum of one-third of the space empty for expansion into ice cream. Fit the cover to the can securely.

3. Place the filled can in the empty tub, making certain that it rests properly in the center.

4. Look on the underside of the power unit to check the location of the deep socket. It is about 1 inch from the surface. The dasher stem is usually flat or square and fits this socket. Position the stem so that when you lower the power unit over it, they fit together. The power unit arms may rest on top of the bucket. If not, wiggle the cover slightly until the power unit drops down that extra ½ inch. Arms on the power unit are then secured to the edges of the bucket. Some twist into place, others slip into special holes, and some have latches or screws that must be tightened securely.

5. Start the unit turning before packing it with ice and salt; it must be moving freely.

6. There will be three evenly distributed layers of ice and salt. The first layer is ice to a height of about one-third of the distance between the bottom of the bucket and the drain hole. Then, evenly sprinkle the first portion of salt over the entire surface of the ice. Repeat this procedure two more times. Your third layer of salt should come just below the drain hole in the side of the tub. This hole should be left open at all times for drainage of excess brine (salt and water). It should be checked at intervals.

7. Pour a cup of cold water evenly over the top layer of salt. (Increase this amount to 1½ cups and 2 cups for the 4-quart and 6-quart freezers.) The top layer of ice

will move down quickly, as it starts to melt. Add more ice to the level of the can cover.

8. After 15 minutes the ice level will probably have dropped again and you should add more ice. By this time the water level will have risen and brine will be coming out the drain hole. A plastic basin under the freezer or other provision to catch this water will save puddle problems.

9. On the average, complete churning is finished in 20–30 minutes. Variations may be due to the sweetness and consistency of different mixes as well as ice-salt ratios. The completion time can best be determined when you hear the motor labor or stop or when the mixture becomes too hard to turn in a hand-crank model. Sometimes—especially if you are using a small amount of mix—there will be no such sign, and you will have to look inside the can. If the mixture has mounded up around the dasher, it is finished even though the motor is still turning.

Electric freezing usually takes longer than hand freezing. As soon as there is resistance in hand freezing, speed up the turning until it is too difficult to turn. The mixture can be finished more quickly and will be a little lighter than the mix produced by the steady turn of the electric freezer.*

10. Unplug the motorized freezer immediately. Loosen and lift the power unit from the freezer. Remove the canister from the bucket. Wipe the cover then the outside with a cold wet sponge. A good check is to rub your finger over the top and sides of the cover and taste it to make sure there is no salt remaining. Remove the cover. Pull up the dasher slowly, gripping it firmly. With a rubber spatula, scrape ice cream back into the can. If the dasher slips back or any ice cream gets on the outside, it may be too salty to eat. Cover the top of

* Note: People doing hand-mixing will stop at various times depending on strength and endurance.

the ice cream with waxed paper or plastic wrap to exclude air. Replace cover and plug the cover hole with the cork.

IF IT DOESN'T FREEZE . . .

Fortunately, frozen desserts respond well to doctoring. If your mix has not frozen in the prescribed time, it may be possible to give it a boost or step up the freezing action by one of the following methods:

Pour off some water through the drain hole and add a few handfuls of salt and a layer of ice. You may have used too little salt or the ice may not have been crushed fine enough.

If you have no success within the next 15 minutes, then stir into the mix 2 beaten egg whites per quart of mix and continue freezing.

Finally, if the mix still is too loose, the only thing left to do is to take it out, warm it, and combine with it an envelope of dissolved gelatin for each two quarts of milk. Chill for half an hour and refreeze.

An excess of fruit acid or too much sweetener may be the reason your mixture does not freeze properly. It may also be possible that your freezer tub leaks and the brine level is too low, preventing the efficient cold transfer to the mix.

IF IT FREEZES TOO SOON . . .

If the freezer action stops or the motor is having a hard time turning within a few minutes after you have started freezing, it may be that the mix is too thick. In that case, the simplest way to loosen it is to stir in some milk. Start with a quarter of a cup per quart of mix and continue adding milk until freezing action resumes normally.

It may be necessary to remove some excess mixture when you add milk so that there is still the proper amount of expansion room in the can.

If you use too much salt with the ice, your mix will have a coarse texture and will not be as smooth as it should be. It will also cause a crust of frozen ice cream to form on the inside of the can, which could force the motor to stop.

Serving

Many people serve ice cream immediately after making it because they love its soft texture, just like the popular soft ice cream served directly from a machine. The taste is fresh and the cream melts in your mouth. It also melts more quickly on your plate. You can keep the ice cream in this pleasant state for a little while by placing the covered can back in the bucket with the used ice and salty water.

Homemade ice cream, sherbets, and ices are best when eaten the same day they are made. When stored for long periods, they develop ice crystals and become brittle.

Ice cream is hardened or firmed to improve its flavor and texture. The standard method of firming in the bucket is as follows:

1. Drain off half the brine.

2. Place the canister back in the bucket.

3. Pack the 2-quart bucket with one cup of salt and more ice in layers to the drain hole. (larger-size freezers require additional salt.) Then cover the canister completely with ice.

4. Surround the entire bucket with plastic, newspapers, burlap, or towels and set it aside to stand in a cool place.

5. Note the time of starting on a card, and place it on top of the covered bucket. The usual firming time is 1 to 3 hours.

6. When firm, the ice cream is ready to be served or stored.

If you wish to avoid the standard method of firming described above, place the covered canister directly in your freezer. It will become firm for serving in an hour or two, or it can be stored in the freezer can.

If you are going to churn another mixture immediately, take the following steps: Remove the ice cream from the canister after the dasher has been taken out, place it in freezer containers, and let it harden in your home freezer. Leave a little air space inside for expansion. Drain off the brine, save the ice, and throw away the salt. Wash the can, dasher, and cover in hot soapy water. Rinse with cold water and you will be ready for the next batch.

Storing

You may store ice cream in the freezer can if you wish. Preferably, you should transfer it (or what is left after serving) to a container that can be tightly sealed. To avoid crystallization, don't forget the wax paper or plastic wrap on the top of the ice cream. Air will also change the flavor.

Empty milk or cream cartons, plastic freezer containers, or containers from commercial ice creams are excellent for storage. Also, round paper containers in pint and quart sizes are available in many stores and specialty paper supply houses.

For best results, chill containers in the freezer before filling them.

You may want to use some of the shaped metal molds, like the heart used for the popular dessert Coeur á la Creme. Metal takes longer to cool. Cupcake baking pans can be fun for children.

For children, plastic freezer pop sets are favorites that work nicely with ices and sherbets. They also like individual paper cups or ice cube trays with tooth picks or paper cupcake holders. Children also enjoy folding their own small aluminum containers.

Plastic parfait sets can be used for freezing and serving. The cover becomes the base. You can use these most imaginatively and combine flavors. Almost any plastic or metal container with or without swizzle sticks is fun.

If you are storing several desserts, it is best to label and date them. For metal or plastic containers, you will need stick-on labels.

Homemade ice creams may become harder than commercial brands in the same freezer. (They have no additives that act like antifreeze.) Storage temperatures should be 0°F. or colder, and be maintained uniformly.

Ice cream is at its best in the first week after it is made. If it is stored for more than one month, it loses its original texture and flavor. (If spices have been used, they will become much too strong.)

Wrapping storage containers of ice cream in aluminum foil aids in prolonged storage.

FROM THE FREEZER TO THE TABLE

Ice cream, sherbets, and ices should not be eaten when they arc frozen solid. If they cannot be easily scooped for serving, they are too hard to eat. When you remove the dessert from storage to serve it, place it in the lower section of the refrigerator for 20–60 minutes to enhance the flavor and soften it. It should yield to spoon pressure when served. If the top layer is dark, the discoloration is due to oxidation and the layer should be removed. It only serves as a natural seal to protect the mixture underneath. Any ice crystals that have formed should also be removed. The metal shortening and ice cream spoons on the market make this job easier.

When you become a serious ice cream buff, you may wish to consider making an important addition to your flatware. You can purchase some special ice cream forks that are simply marvelous; they are shovel-shaped spoons with broad tines.

If your dessert is not too firmly frozen, try chilling the serving dishes in the freezer for five minutes.

One cup of sauce or topping is usually enough for six servings. However, most desserts are so good that people usually want seconds, so be prepared.

CLEANING YOUR FREEZER

1. Wash the can, dasher, and cover in hot, soapy water immediately after use. (Although it is best to use the hottest water to clean any cooking equipment, freezer parts should not be put in the dishwasher because the temperature is too high.) Dry thoroughly before storing. Place the cork in a small plastic bag inside the can so that it is not misplaced.

2. Empty brine and ice solution from the bucket, then thoroughly flush it with clear water. Wipe outside and inside with a damp cloth to remove any excess salt solution.

3. Clean the motor frame with a wet cloth, but do not immerse it in water. Particularly, wipe all traces of salt and moisture from metal parts.

4. Store the unit in a cool dry place.

Part 2

The Recipes

What's Cooking

Considerations for each recipe were:

● Proper blending for the most enjoyable taste; therefore, some have a little more or less mix and yield.

● Churning for no more than half an hour; waiting for the good stuff is tough enough.

● Producing approximately 1 quart to 1½ quarts of finished ice cream, sherbet, or ice—or 10–12 medium- to good-size portions; this way, you can easily figure how much to make.

All the recipes in this book can easily be increased to fit the size of your own freezer. However, it may be necessary to adjust individual flavorings to your personal taste rather than to merely double or triple them as you do the other ingredients. You cannot determine what the final taste of the ice cream will be by the initial tasting of the mix before freezing. The coldness of the frozen product dulls the taste buds. For this reason, the mix always tastes overly sweet and flavorful before freezing. It is, therefore, suggested that you try a particular recipe as directed first, then makes notes on your personal taste as a guide for the next time.

Many recipes specify using a blender to combine soft ingredients. This was done for ease and convenience as well as speed. If you wish, they can, of course, be mixed by hand.

ALMOND ICE CREAM

4 egg yolks
½ c. honey
pinch salt
1 c. light cream

¾ c. heavy cream
½ lb. blanched almonds
2 t. almond extract

1. Beat egg yolks and mix with honey and salt in top of double boiler.
2. Add light cream to honey mixture and cook, stirring constantly, until mixture coats a spoon. Cool.
3. Whip heavy cream lightly.
4. Chop almonds finely.
5. Add whipped cream, chopped almonds, and almond extract to cooled honey mixture.
6. Churn-freeze.

You may have liked almonds before, but hated all that chewing. But now we've made it easy for you—and featured them in this light, crunchy creation.

Almonds, like most nuts, are an especially rich source of protein and the B vitamins.

If you have to blanch your own almonds, it's a relatively simple job: Cover them with cold water and bring to a boil. Let them cool, take them out of the water, and remove the skins easily by placing the almonds between your thumb and forefinger.

Meringue Topping

The spare egg whites will keep in the refrigerator in a lidded jar for about two weeks. Use them for a meringue or add to omelets for extra fluffiness. For a simple meringue topping that is great for any dessert: Beat 2 egg whites with ⅛ teaspoon salt until stiff, then gradually beat in ½ cup of raw sugar until glossy.

One tablespoon of honey per egg white also makes a delicious meringue.

APPLE CREAM

3 medium apples
1½ c. heavy cream
⅓ c. honey

½ T. lemon juice
pinch salt

1. Peel, core, and dice apples.
2. Combine apples, cream, honey, lemon juice, and salt. Mix until completely blended.
3. Churn-freeze.

The joy of this particular combination is that the diced pieces of apple stand out a bit from the creamy mixture. This gives a crunchiness and texture difference that delights everyone.

This is an all-year-round favorite since apples are always available. Varieties that can be used for many purposes are: *Wealthy* (tart and spicy), *Jonathan* (spicy and juicy), *Grimes Golden* (bland and sweet), *Cortland* (mild and spicy), *Golden Delicious* (rich, sweet and firm, an interesting sweet taste), *Stayman* (rich and winy), *York* (tart and firm), *Baldwin* (mild and firm), *Northern Spy* (tender and spicy), and *Newton Pippin* (tart and crisp). Try your own favorite.

Don't use *Greenings* left over from your pie baking: they require far too much sweetener.

Remember, all apples must be stored in a cold, dry place.

APPLESAUCE CIDER SHERBET

1 env. unflavored gelatin
½ c. water
1½ c. applesauce

1½ c. cider
6 T. raw sugar
1 T. lemon juice

1. In a double boiler soften gelatin in water; stir over hot, not boiling, water, until gelatin is dissolved.
2. Combine dissolved gelatin, applesauce, cider, sugar, and lemon juice; mix well.
3. Churn-freeze.

A wonderful way to help you get your "apple-a-day," and it is a frosty, thirst-quenching delight.

You will find the flavor much more satisfying if you use homemade applesauce. Don't be afraid of using spices, provided that the dessert is to be eaten shortly after it is made; otherwise, those spices will tend to dominate. We've cooked our applesauce with cracked ginger and then strained it—the zest of the ginger really enhances the apple's mellow flavor.

For a truly different taste, add ½ cup of puréed apricots and use only 1 cup of applesauce; these 2 fruits produce a blend of flavor that is just right.

APRICOT ALMOND TEMPTATION

1 c. dried apricots
1½ c. water
1 T. refined oil
¼ c. raw sugar
½ c. chopped, blanched almonds

½ c. crunchy granola
½ t. almond extract
1 t. vanilla
2 eggs
1½ c. raw milk
½ c. half and half

1. Simmer the apricots and water together in a small saucepan until tender. This usually takes about 15–20 minutes. Remove from heat and drain the juice off, saving ½ cup of it. Purée apricots with the half cup of juice. Set aside.

2. Combine oil, sugar, almonds, and granola in top of a double boiler. Cook, stirring occasionally, until the mixture is thoroughly blended. Remove from heat. Cool.

3. Mix crumb mixture with puréed apricots. Add almond extract and vanilla.

4. Beat eggs well and combine with milk and half and half.

5. Stir apricot crumb mixture into egg-milk combination.

6. Churn-freeze.

A flavorful, crunchy dish that makes a delectable dessert—a real treat for those ice cream lovers who get their kicks from sweet surprises. Though the apricots, like all other dried fruits, are a great source of natural sugar, we added a little bit of raw sugar for freezing purposes. It enhances this dessert's rich flavor.

Almonds, like most nuts, are really an ancient food. They are mentioned in the Old Testament more than 70 times and still are produced in the Biblical regions and other parts of the Near East, France, Italy, Spain, and Mediterranean area. Noted for their flavor and versatility, almonds are one of the best of all nuts and are a rich source of protein. Apricots, too, are a beneficial addition to anyone's diet.

APRICOT MOUSSE CREAM

1 orange
½ lb. sun-dried apricots
¼ c. lemon juice
¼ c. finely chopped,
  blanched almonds

1 c. yogurt
pinch salt
¼ c. honey
1½ c. half and half
½ c. heavy cream

1. Slice the orange, including the skin, into thin pieces.

2. Place apricots, sliced orange, lemon juice, and almonds in the top of a double boiler. Cook over low heat until soft. If necessary, add a small amount of water to prevent mixture from becoming too thick.

3. Purée apricot-orange mixture in a blender or food mill.

4. Combine with the rest of the ingredients and mix until smooth and creamy. Chill.

5. Churn-freeze.

A marvelous combination—almost a mousse, but really an ice cream. The natural sweetness of the apricots and the zest of the orange produce an unusual flavor that lingers on the tongue long after eating.

For a change of taste and consistency, remember that yogurt, buttermilk, and sour cream may be used interchangeably, in this recipe as well as many others.

Special note: Since this is a mousse cream, it will not harden in the same way that regular ice cream does; therefore, the motor may not be stopped when it is completed. You may just hear it labor.

AVOCADO DELIGHT

1 medium-size ripe
  avocado
2½ T. lime juice
⅓ c. honey
½ c. natural raspberry
  preserves

4 T. finely chopped,
  preserved ginger
pinch sea salt
1 c. heavy cream
½ c. light cream

1. Cut avocado in half, peel, and purée in an electric blender or food mill. Combine avocado purée with lime juice, honey, raspberry preserves, ginger, and salt. Blend until smooth.

2. Whip cream lightly and fold into avocado mixture. Chill.

3. Churn-freeze.

A marvelous medley of interesting tastes—quite exotic. As an extra dividend, there are pits for cultivating those great plants.

This rich, mildly flavored fruit must be completely ripe, which means that it is mellow, soft, and yields readily to gentle pressure. Avocados are generally at their peak from February through April.

If you do not intend to use this dessert within a day or two after making, reduce the ginger to 2 tablespoons.

Avocado Dressing

If you find that you have too much mix for your freezer, leftover mix makes an excellent dressing for your favorite fruit salad.

AVOCADO LIME ICE CREAM

1 medium-size ripe avocado	2 t. grated lime rind
⅔ c. raw sugar	½ c. pineapple juice
3½ T. lime juice	½ t. salt
	2 c. light cream

1. Cut avocado in half, peel, and mash.
2. Combine mashed avocado, sugar, lime juice and rind, pineapple juice, salt, and cream in bowl; blend until smooth. Chill.
3. Churn-freeze.

Avocados and limes are one of those rare combinations—subtle perfection. You'll agree with that statement once you taste this lovely, light-green ice cream. (The refreshing lime taste absorbs the oil content of the avocado.) Serve either as dessert or with a salad.

Strawberry Topping

If you have any strawberries in the refrigerator that you didn't serve because of blemishes or discoloration, wash and hull and put them in the blender with your favorite whipping cream. Makes a particularly colorful topping.

AVOCADO PECAN ICE CREAM

1 t. unflavored gelatin	½ c. honey
1 T. water	pinch sea salt
2 ripe avocados	2 c. heavy cream
2 T. lemon juice	½ c. chopped pecans

1. Soften gelatin in water in top of double boiler for 5 minutes. Heat and stir until dissolved.

2. Cut avocado in half, peel, and purée pulp in an electric blender or food mill. While puréeing, add lemon juice, honey, and salt to the avocado pulp.

3. Whip cream lightly and combine with dissolved gelatin, avocado mixture, and pecans. Blend until smooth.

4. Churn-freeze.

Avocado aficionados cannot afford to overlook this colorful dark-green dessert. They will thrill to the unexpected taste of the puréed avocado when blended with chewy pecans in a cool dessert.

Even though avocados are fruits, we tend to use them as vegetables; therefore, it's great to be able to have them for dessert, especially since they are a source of the essential fatty acids that prominent health food nutritionists consider so vital to the diet.

To vary the flavor and reduce the strong flavor of the avocado, a half cup of small-curd cottage cheese can be puréed with the avocado.

BANANA CUSTARD ICE CREAM

1 c. milk	1 pt. light cream
½ c. honey	1 T. vanilla
4 T. whole-wheat flour	2 bananas
3 eggs	1 T. lemon juice
⅛ t. salt	

1. Heat milk in the top of a double boiler, reserving three tablespoons. Do not allow to boil.

2. Make a paste of the honey, flour, and reserved milk. Add to the milk in the double boiler.

3. Beat eggs with salt and combine with 2 tablespoons of the milk mixture.

4. Stir in beaten eggs to the hot milk mixture and continue cooking, stirring constantly until smooth and creamy.

5. Pour hot milk mixture in to mixing bowl; add cream and vanilla.

6. Cool.

7. Mash bananas finely and blend with lemon juice.

8. Combine mashed bananas with cooled custard mixture.

9. Churn-freeze.

Full of goodness and supersmooth richness—a wonderful way to have frozen bananas. If the bananas are too ripe, the flavor will be stronger and the color darker. Try it topped with crumbled wafers. If available, use soy flour to boost the nutritive content of this delicious dessert.

BANANA NUT BREAD ICE CREAM

¼ c. honey
pinch salt
2 egg yolks, slightly beaten
1 c. light cream

¾ c. banana nut bread
   crumbs
1¼ c. heavy cream
½ t. vanilla

1. Stir honey, salt, and slightly beaten egg yolks together until well mixed.

2. Put mixture in top of double boiler, add light cream, and cook, stirring constantly, until mixture coats a spoon. Cool.

3. Crumble banana nut bread between two slices of wax paper to obtain crumbs. Soak crumbs in heavy cream for 5 minutes.

4. Add vanilla and banana nut bread crumbs in cream to egg yolk mixture.

5. Churn-freeze.

A sweet, smooth, natural-tasting ice cream with mild crumbly texture. The banana bread should be one of the firmer bread types; if it is more like a cake, add to the cream and eliminate soaking time. Other tasty breads such as date and nut, raisin, carrot, carob, apricot, or apple may be used. For any one of these breads, you may want to add pieces of the appropriate fruit or vegetable to step up the taste. Or you may want to serve with pieces of the fruit as decorative touches on the ice cream. Also, don't forget that macaroons can be substituted for bread.

BERRY ICE (Nero's Pleasure)

1 pt. fresh berries	¼ c. orange or lemon
¾ c. honey	juice
¾ c. water	

1. Wash and purée berries in a food mill or blender. Strain through a fine sieve or strainer to remove seeds.
2. Combine honey and water into a syrup and boil over a low heat until thoroughly mixed. Cool.
3. Blend puréed berries, honey syrup, and juice.
4. Churn-freeze.

A pleasing simple dessert. It is equally good when made with any of the following berries: raspberries, blackberries, blueberries, strawberries, gooseberries, huckleberries, currants, or dewberries. Generally all berries are perishable and can be held for only a few days in the refrigerator. Keep them cold, dry, and whole to retain their nutrients. Do not handle them in any way until you are actually using them. (When using berries, wash off everything they touch immediately, as they sometimes tend to stain.)

We have dedicated this ice to Roman Emperor Nero Claudis Caesar (A.D. 54—68), as many historians claim that he was responsible for the first frozen dessert ever created. Satisfying his gustatory pleasures was an exhausting passion, and his legions were ordered to bring back fresh snow from the mountains, to which he added fruit juices and other flavorings to titillate his palate. In those days keeping ice was so difficult that only an emperor could afford this self-indulgence.

BLACKBERRY SHERBET

1 c. blackberries, fresh or frozen	juice of 1 orange
	¼ c. honey
juice of 1 lemon	2½ c. milk

1. Purée fresh blackberries in a blender or food mill. If using frozen berries, sprinkle with ¼ c. raw sugar and partially thaw, following directions on package, then purée.
2. Combine berries with the other ingredients and blend until smooth. Chill.
3. Churn-freeze

A tart, tantalizing taste makes this a special sherbet full of zip and zest. Blackberries, also known as brambles, are a firm plump berry with a rich, dark color. They should be used as soon as possible after being picked or purchased.

Blueberries or raspberries may be substituted in any recipe that calls for blackberries.

Rainbow Parfait

Try this one in a rainbow parfait. Alternate layers of blackberry sherbet between orange and lime sherbets. Top with your favorite whipped cream and sliced strawberries. Try using plastic parfait glasses (their bases can be used as covers) to make some extras for after-school snacks.

BLEU CHEESE BONANZA

5 oz. grated bleu cheese	1 c. milk
3 oz. cream cheese	pinch sea salt
pinch minced onion flakes	¼ t. raw sugar
1 T. lemon juice	2 c. sour cream

1. Combine bleu cheese, cream cheese, onion flakes, lemon juice, and milk in the top of a double boiler. Cook, stirring frequently, until the cheese and milk are thoroughly blended. Cool.

2. Add salt, sugar, and sour cream to the cooled cheese mixture; blend until smooth and creamy.

3. Churn-freeze.

The subtle taste and texture of this mix make it a marvelous salad dressing straight from the bowl. With freezing, something special happens . . . a rich and distinctive garnish with a tingly taste that provides a gala touch to crisp greens, fresh fruits, or mixed vegetable salads.

If you want to substitute Gorgonzola cheese, use 6 ounces and only 2 ounces of cream cheese. Both these mold-ripened, crumbly cheeses (Gorgonzola and bleu) are classified as semihard cheeses. (All natural cheeses, regardless of their individual characteristics, are classified into three basic types: soft, semihard, and hard.)

BLUEBERRY ICE CREAM

1 env. unflavored gelatin	2 c. sour cream
½ c. water	1 T. maple syrup
½ c. honey	1 T. grated orange rind
1 pt. fresh blueberries	½ t. cinnamon
pinch sea salt	1 c. heavy cream

1. Soften gelatin in water for 5 minutes.

2. Combine gelatin with honey in top of double boiler and cook over hot water, stirring constantly, for about 10 minutes, or until gelatin is completely dissolved. Turn off heat.

3. Purée blueberries and add to honey mixture; resume cooking, on medium heat, stirring constantly, for an additional 10 minutes. Cool.

4. Add salt, sour cream, maple syrup, orange rind, and cinnamon to blueberry mixture; blend until smooth.

5. Lightly whip heavy cream and fold into blueberry mixture.

6. Churn-freeze.

Be sure to try this flavorsome dessert for your July 4 festivities. (Those bright blue berries with a slightly frosted look are most plentiful in July.) Cultivated berries are larger than wild berries, but it's the wild ones that have the finer flavor. For out-of-season serving, frozen natural blueberries without sugar are easily available in most supermarkets as well as health food stores and specialty food shops.

Very few of us realize that a cup of fresh blueberries will provide one-third of the adult daily requirement of vitamin C.

Slim Jim Topping

With so many goodies on hand for the holiday celebration, serve with a Slim Jim Topping made as follows: Take ½ cup evaporated skim milk, place in bowl in which you intend to whip it, and refrigerate until thoroughly chilled. Remove from refrigerator and beat until the mixture holds stiff peaks. Fold in 1 tablespoon raw sugar and serve immediately, as it doesn't have the staying power of whipped cream.

For a red, white, and blue touch, add sliced strawberries in the center of the topping when you spoon it on the blue ice cream.

BUTTER PECAN ICE CREAM

½ c. finely chopped pecans
2 T. butter
1½ c. heavy cream

½ c. honey
1 T. vanilla
1 c. milk

1. Lightly brown the pecans in the butter. Dry the nuts on a piece of paper toweling to drain off the excess butter. Cool.
2. Combine the buttered pecans, cream, honey, vanilla, and milk.
3. Churn-freeze.

Vive le beurre. Vive les pecans. Vive les glaces. How could we complete this book without including a luscious, creamy butter pecan? We turned to the French to salute it, and we'll borrow a French idea for serving: a coupe. In France, coupes are usually served in champagne-type glasses. However, any stemmed glass may be used. Coupes can be garnished with whipped cream, candied fruit, chopped nuts, candied flowers, mint leaves, or chopped, fresh fruit.

Coupe Natural

A rare treat for summer entertaining. Top butter pecan ice cream with fresh sweetened blueberries and garnish with whipped cream and crushed pecans.

To return to practical matters, do not purchase butter that is not dated. If you don't understand the coding used in your supermarket or dairy, ask the manager to explain it. Fresh sweet butter is a pure delight, but it must be fresh. Butter is a nutritious food, containing vitamin A, lecithin, and other growth-promoting substances that unfortunately are not present in butter substitutes.

BUTTERMILK SHERBET

¼ c. honey
1 c. puréed, unsweetened fruit
1½ c. buttermilk

1 T. lemon or lime juice
grated rind of 1 lemon or lime
2 egg whites

1. Combine honey, puréed fruit, buttermilk, juice, and rind in mixing bowl. Blend until smooth. Chill.
2. Beat egg whites until soft peaks form.
3. Fold egg whites into buttermilk mixture.
4. Churn-freeze.

An elegant and easy dessert—good as is, but extra good if you add half a cup of apricot, cherry, grape, orange, pineapple, peach, raspberry, or strawberry juice. Oranges or pineapples do wonderful things for this sherbet. A really tingling variation is puréed blueberries with lime juice.

Making Your Own Buttermilk

Be creative and try making your own buttermilk. Mix ½ cup buttermilk into 4 cups of milk and cover. Allow mixture to stand at room temperature until it is thickened. Refrigerate, if you are not going to use immediately. Keep ½ cup as your "starter" for a fresh supply.

BUTTERSCOTCH PECAN PUDDING ICE CREAM

1 4-oz. package natural butterscotch pudding	¼ t. almond extract
1 3-inch piece vanilla bean	2 c. heavy cream
	1 c. chopped pecans

1. Prepare pudding according to instructions on package, using half of the amount of milk required. While it is cooking, add vanilla bean to mix. Cook only until mixture begins to thicken. Remove from heat and let cool for 10 minutes. Discard vanilla bean.

2. Add almond extract and heavy cream.

3. Churn-freeze.

4. Add nuts, mixing lightly throughout.

Most ice creams are good; however, this one is great. It's sweet, heavenly rich, and crunchy—the vanilla bean adds that extraspecial gourmet flavor.

Here's your chance to turn a packaged pudding containing natural ingredients into an ice cream the easy way. These natural puddings also come in other flavors such as carob and plain vanilla.

If the butterscotch taste is not strong enough for you, add some carmelized sugar. Simply melt 3 tablespoons of butter in a heavy skillet at low heat; add 1 cup of raw sugar and continue to cook, stirring constantly, for

5 minutes. Add ¼ cup of water to keep it from hardening. Cool, and add as much as you think is necessary to the mix before you churn it.

Any vanilla recipe can be converted into butterscotch pecan simply by adding the pecans and carmelized sugar. Pecans are an especially versatile ingredient in cooking and are one of our most popular and valuable nuts.

CANTALOUPE ICE

1 large ripe cantaloupe	½ c. honey
2 c. water	¾ T. lemon juice

1. Cut cantaloupe in half, remove seeds and rind, and purée in a blender or food mill. Set aside.
2. Combine water and honey in top of a double boiler and heat for 5 minutes. Cool.
3. Add cantaloupe pulp and lemon juice to honey syrup. Mix well.
4. Churn-freeze.

A scrumptious way to end a summer meal. The melon should have a slight "give" when you press it gently, but don't confuse this springiness with softness. A smooth stem end of the melon and a fragrant aroma indicate its ripeness. Unripe melons usually need about a day or two on a sunny window ledge to ripen. The lemon juice accentuates and enhances the melon's flavor.

If you like, try this recipe with a honeydew melon and lime juice. Taste the mix before churn-freezing; it may require additional honey.

CANTALOUPE ICE CREAM

1 large ripe cantaloupe
½ pt. heavy cream
½ c. honey
¼ t. salt
1 t. vanilla

¼ t. almond extract
¼ c. milk
6 T. fresh lemon juice
1 pt. half and half

1. Cut cantaloupe in half; remove seeds and rind. Mash well and purée in food mill or electric blender.
2. Add remaining ingredients and mix well.
3. Churn-freeze.

Sweet and light. Perfect at any time of day. Really delicious with sliced strawberries. If desired, lime juice may be substituted for the lemon juice to add extra zest and emphasize the delicacy of the melon's flavor. Great way to use those overripe cantaloupes.

If you would like the taste of the cantaloupe to stand out from the creamy mixture, add three tablespoons of finely diced cantaloupe to the mix after it is churn-frozen. You will then have eye appeal with that distinctive cantaloupe flavor.

CAROB ICE CREAM

2 c. milk
3-inch piece of vanilla
    bean
4 egg yolks

½ c. honey
1 c. carob powder
¾ c. hot water
2 c. heavy cream

1. Combine milk and vanilla bean in top of double boiler; heat until mixture just comes to a boil.
2. Mix egg yolks and honey and beat with a wire whisk in a medium-size mixing bowl for 3 minutes.

3. Discard vanilla bean from double boiler and pour hot milk slowly into beaten egg yolks. Beat gently.

4. Pour mixture back into double boiler and cook over low heat, stirring constantly, until mixture thickens to a custard that coats the spoon. Do not allow to boil.

5. Mix carob powder with hot water. Add to mixture in double boiler.

6. When mixture becomes a custardy consistency, remove from heat and cool. Add cream.

7. Churn-freeze.

A deep, chocolately flavor for chocolate lovers who perfer "natural carob." This is a wonderful mineral-rich, quick-energy, satisfying dessert. For a lighter flavor, use 6 tablespoons carob powder with 4 tablespoons of hot water.

Vanilla Soy Topping

For extra nutrition, try a whipped cream topping you can fix in a minute. Put ½ cup soy milk, ½ cup refined oil, 1 tablespoon honey, ¼ teaspoon vanilla, and a pinch of sea salt in your blender—that's it.

CAROB MINT ICE CREAM

2 c. milk	3 eggs
12-oz. carob bar	⅔ c. honey
3 T. carob powder	2 c. heavy cream
1 T. fresh peppermint leaves	1 T. vanilla
	⅛ t. salt

1. Combine milk, carob bar, carob powder, and mint leaves in top of double boiler and cook over hot, not boiling, water until thick and smooth. Cool.

2. Beat eggs and blend with honey. Add heavy

cream, vanilla, and salt; mix until smooth and creamy.

3. Strain carob mixture in order to discard mint leaves—the flavor has been released.

4. Add strained carob mixture to egg mixture and blend thoroughly.

5. Churn-freeze.

Marvelous, exciting, refreshing minty chocolate taste. The carob bar should be tasted first to make sure that it is fresh. When you buy, look for those bars that are double-wrapped; it really makes a difference in the taste.

Add ¼ cup of walnuts and raisins after churn-freezing for an interesting variation.

For a unique "spicy" carob taste, eliminate peppermint leaves and add ½ teaspoon of cinnamon and a pinch of nutmeg.

CAROB MOCHA Á LA MODE

1 env. unflavored gelatin	2 egg yolks, beaten
¼ c. water	¾ c. raw sugar
2 c. milk	2 egg whites, beaten stiff
½ c. Tiger's Milk, plain	1 T. vanilla
3 T. carob powder	1 T. grated orange rind
2 T. brewed, decaffeinated coffee	

1. Soften gelatin in water until dissolved. Set aside.

2. Combine milk with powdered dry milk in top of double boiler over hot water, stirring constantly until water is boiling.

3. Stir in carob powder and coffee; blend well.

4. Mix egg yolks with a little of the hot mixture and add to the milk mixture.

5. Add sugar, mixing until creamy.

6. Add gelatin. Remove from heat. Cool.

7. Mix in vanilla, and orange rind.
8. Fold in egg whites.
9. Churn-freeze.

An exciting blend whose distinctive flavors complement each other most invitingly. We could call it "chocolate" mocha in an attempt to deceive you, but why should we? Once you try it, all those chocolate cravings will disappear—and you'll want to use this wonderful natural carob all the time. The carob bean is about 50 percent natural sugar and is a natural source of calcium, phosphorous, potassium, and a host of other important minerals and vitamins.

Carob Curl Topping

The ice cream alone is sensational; however, for an extrasuper dessert, garnish with your favorite whipped topping and jumbo carob curls for decoration. For the curls, use a plain carob bar and a vegetable parer. Holding the parer flat, draw the blade across the candy bar—the curls will roll up very nicely.

CARROT RAISIN ICE CREAM

1½ c. sliced carrots	1 c. half and half
¼ c. honey	2 egg whites
1 T. fresh spearmint leaves	1 T. dried lemon peel
1 c. carrot juice	¼ c. honey
1 T. nonfat dry milk powder	½ c. seedless raisins
pinch sea salt	½ c. heavy cream
1 t. vanilla	

1. Cook carrots with honey and spearmint leaves in a small saucepan over a low heat for about 5 minutes. It may be necessary to add a little water. Remove from

heat and strain the honey syrup to remove the spearmint leaves.

2. Purée carrot-honey mixture and combine with carrot juice, dry milk powder, salt, vanilla, and half and half. Blend until smooth. Cool.

3. Beat egg whites lightly and stir into honey and dried lemon peel.

4. Mix honey and egg white mixture with cooled carrots.

5. Add heavy cream and raisins.

6. Churn-freeze.

A make-it-yourself pleasing treat for natural food lovers. Sweet and zesty, too. Desserts like this may be the start of an ice cream renaissance. Fifty years ago the hand-cranked freezer was as common an item in anyone's kitchen as the electric blender is today.

George Washington is actually credited with being one of America's earliest ice cream enthusiasts. Aside from all her other duties, the ever-faithful Martha always had to keep two pewter ice cream pots at hand (the favorite equipment at that time for turning out successful ice cream). It is truly a "presidential passion"; most of Washington's successors have disagreed on many items but concurred in their fondness for ice cream. Dolly Madison served it at the Inaugural Ball in 1809 and other presidents often had ice cream for dessert.

CASHEWNUTTY CREME

½ c. milk
½ c. half and half
pinch sea salt
⅔ c. cashew nut butter
2 t. vanilla
½ t. almond extract
1 t. cinnamon
¼ c. honey
1 T. wheat germ
2 c. heavy cream
1 c. chopped, natural cashew nuts

1. Mix all ingredients except chopped cashew nuts and cream in blender until smooth. Add heavy cream.
2. Churn-freeze.
3. After removal from the freezer, add chopped nuts—mixing lightly throughout.

A crunchy nougat delight that is crisp and chewy-perfect. Cashew nuts are most wholesome and nutritious when eaten unroasted, and are a welcome addition to a good natural diet.

Raspberry Sauce Topping

For a superb indulgence, fill half a cantaloupe with a scoop of this ice cream and top with raspberry sauce (homemade, of course).

Wash and force 1 pint of raspberries through a food mill or a fine sieve. Add ½ cup honey and mix well. Bring to a boil over medium heat, stirring until a heavy syrup is formed.

CHEESE-YOGURT SHERBET

1½ c. cottage cheese	¼ t. ginger
1½ c. yogurt	¼ t. cinnamon
¼ c. honey	½ c. heavy cream
½ t. dried orange peel	1 T. wheat germ
½ t. dried lemon peel	1 T. vanilla
½ T. lemon juice	

1. Combine all ingredients in blender until smooth.
2. Churn-freeze.

Those of you who are daily cottage cheese and yogurt addicts will find this a melt-in-the-mouth, sure-to-please dessert.

Instead of the dried orange and lemon peel, a teaspoon of powdered fruit rind could be substituted.

Powdered fruit rind is a combination of orange, lemon, and grapefruit rinds; it can easily be made in your own kitchen. When stored in a tightly sealed jar, it keeps indefinitely.

How to Make Powdered Fruit Rinds

Wash and dry the fruit; cut thin sections of rind from each. Place in a pan and dry in a warm place. Make sure they're thoroughly dry and then pulverize in a blender. Put through a fine sieve and if there are any pieces remaining in the sieve, put them back in the blender again.

If your blender doesn't have a pulverizing cycle, use an old-fashioned standing grater, switching sides from coarse to fine so that you obtain the right texture. The flavorful part of the rind is the thin outer surface, the part that carries the color.

Crunchy Apple Sauce Topping

Served with a warm Crunchy Apple Sauce Topping, this turns into a real sweet-tooth satisfier. Heat 1 cup chopped peeled apples, 1 cup maple syrup, and a pinch of sea salt to a boil. Simmer about 5 minutes, or until the apples are tender. Then add ¼ cup of your favorite crunchy granola. Stir well and serve warm on sherbet.

CHERRY ICE CREAM

2½ c. tart pitted cherries	1½ T. arrowroot
pinch sea salt	2 T. lemon juice
¼ c. honey	2 t. cinnamon
½ T. vanilla	2 eggs
½ T. almond extract	1 c. goat's milk
¾ c. honey	1 c. goat's heavy cream

1. In a small saucepan cook 2 cups of cherries (reserve ½ cup), sea salt, and honey over a low flame until soft. Purée. Cool.

2. Combine cherries with vanilla, almond extract, honey, arrowroot, lemon juice, cinnamon, eggs, and milk. Blend until smooth.

3. Lightly whip cream and fold into cherry mixture.

4. Chop ½ cup of cherries into small, bite-size pieces and swirl through mixture.

5. Churn-freeze.

This is a lovely, smooth-tasting joy, just perfect with squares of your favorite light, moist pound or sponge cake.

We used frozen cherries; the sour cherries are rarely found in fresh produce markets. The most popular available sweet cherry is the Bing, which is an extra large, heart-shaped fruit with firm, meaty flesh and a luscious flavor. Bings can be used for this recipe and will produce a fine ice cream; however, it may be necessary to reduce the amount of honey from ¾ cup to ½ cup depending upon the taste and sweetness of the natural cherries.

Never use canned cherries; they are usually heavily laden with preservatives and flavored with white sugar.

CHESTNUT FESTIVAL

1½ c. boiled fresh chestnuts
pinch sea salt
½ c. pineapple juice
1½ c. milk
3 egg yolks
½ c. honey
½ c. natural pack crushed
   pineapple
½ c. heavy cream
2 t. vanilla
pinch mace

1. Purée boiled chestnuts with sea salt and pineapple juice. Set aside.

2. In top of double boiler, heat milk until bubbling.

3. Beat egg yolks and honey together. Add 2 table-spoons of hot milk and continue beating. Return combined mixture to double boiler. Cook, stirring frequently, until thickened. Cool.

4. Add chestnut purée, crushed pineapple, heavy cream, vanilla, and mace to the cooled egg-milk mixture. Blend until smooth.

5. Churn-freeze.

Unusual and sublime—subtly sweetened, a dazzling flavor. This is a fabulous holiday dessert providing a rare treat that is delightfully different from the customary traditions. All in all, the perfect way to pay homage to that special dinner.

In many European countries (among them France, Italy, Spain, Switzerland, and Germany), chestnuts are considered a staple food and are much more popular than in the United States. The smell of roasted chestnuts is indeed something special. Make some extras just for munching.

Preparing Chestnuts

Chestnuts are easily shelled as follows: Using a sharp, pointed knife, make two cross-cut gashes on their flat side. Even if the shell comes off when you do this, don't worry, the inner skin protects the kernel. Roast the chestnuts in the oven for 5 minutes at medium temperature. Then steam for 20 minutes. Drain and remove the shells and skin. *Par excellence!*

CINNAMON ICE CREAM

½ c. honey	1 egg yolk
½ c. water	½ t. vanilla
3 cinnamon sticks	1 c. heavy cream
2 c. half and half	½ T. ground cinnamon

1. In a saucepan, mix together honey, water, and cinnamon sticks. Cook the syrup 10 minutes and then remove the cinnamon sticks. Cool.

2. Put half and half in top of double boiler and bring to a boil.

3. Beat egg yolk. Pour a few tablespoons of the hot half and half into the beaten egg yolk. Add the egg mixture to the double boiler. Cook, stirring constantly, until thickened. Cool.

4. Combine cinnamon syrup, vanilla, heavy cream, and ground cinnamon with the cooled egg mixture.

5. Churn-freeze.

How sweet it is! Cinnamon, universally used and enjoyed, was one of the first spices known to man. Has cinnamon been a spice you like in other foods? If so, tasting it alone as a single flavor enhancer will make this an unusual ice cream treat.

Nut Cream Sauce

A simple sauce, easily made, that you might enjoy is whipped up in a minute with your favorite nut butter. All you have to do is blend 1 cup nut butter and ½ cup milk until well mixed and serve.

COCONUT ICE CREAM
(Polynesian Treat)

1 T. vanilla
½ T. arrowroot
¾ c. milk
2 egg yolks
¼ c. honey

pinch sea salt
1¼ c. unsweetened, natural
    shredded coconut
1¼ c. heavy cream

1. In top of a double boiler, mix together vanilla, arrowroot, and milk. Cook for 5 minutes.

2. Beat egg yolks lightly with honey and salt. Add to hot vanilla mixture. Cook, stirring constantly, until thickened. Cool.

3. Add coconut and heavy cream to the cooled mixture.

4. Churn-freeze.

The taste of coconut set in this rich creamy base will be welcome at any time. Top with some crushed pineapple.

The coconut has an interesting history; Marco Polo was one of the first Europeans to discover it. In the many tropical countries where it grows, nearly every part of the tree is utilized. It is also an important staple item of the diet and a vital nutrient wherever it is widely eaten.

If you're using the meat from a fresh coconut, substitute the coconut milk for the regular milk to peak the flavor. Also—for variation—try adding a quarter cup of pineapple juice to the mix.

COMPOTE ICE CREAM

1½ c. dried fruit compote	¾ c. heavy cream
¼ c. orange juice	3 egg yolks
1 t. grated lemon rind	pinch sea salt
¾ c. honey	2 t. vanilla
1¼ c. milk	

1. Purée fruit compote with orange juice, lemon rind, and honey. Set aside.

2. Scald milk and cream in top of a double boiler.

3. Beat egg yolks with salt and combine with two tablespoons of the milk mixture.

4. Stir in beaten eggs to the hot milk mixture and continue cooking, stirring constantly, until thickened. Remove from heat and cool.

5. Combine cooled milk mixture with puréed fruit. Add vanilla and blend until smooth.

6. Churn-freeze.

Those of you who eat dried fruit all the time will really love this frozen version. When serving, drizzle with honey, some yogurt, and a handful of toasted sunflower or sesame seeds.

Fruit Compote

A marvelous natural fruit compote can easily be made as follows: Take ½ cup each of raisins, dried apples, apricots, and prunes; add 4 cups of water, 2 cinnamon sticks, ¼ teaspoon of sea salt, and a pinch of nutmeg. Place all ingredients in a saucepan and cook for 20 minutes over low heat, or until fruit is soft and tender. That's all there is to it.

COTTAGE CHEESE ICE CREAM

2 c. cottage cheese
1 c. fresh milk

2 T. vanilla
¼ c. honey

1. Blend together all ingredients, until smooth and creamy.
2. Churn-freeze.

Quick, easy, inexpensive, versatile, light ice cream.

Taste will depend on the type of cottage cheese you prefer. Cottage cheese is made from skim milk and is usually available in small curd or large curd, either creamed or uncreamed. The curd of the coagulated protein of skim milk is cooked in its own whey, drained, and washed. For creamed cottage cheese, fresh sweet cream is added; uncreamed is drained curd without the addition of cream. We like to use the creamy, small curd. Naturally, if the curd is tart, the final product will be tart also. If the cottage cheese is very sweet, you may want to substitute raw sugar for the honey, so that the taste of the honey will not dominate.

This is an excellent base and can be varied in many ways. Try adding a half cup of your favorite puréed fruit or fruit juice before churn-freezing and create your own special flavors.

CRANAPPLE CONFECTION

1½ c. baked apple purée
½ c. honey
¾ c. cranberry juice
pinch nutmeg

pinch cinnamon
1 c. yogurt
½ c. half and half
1 T. wheat germ

1. Combine baked apple purée with honey and cranberry juice. Mix until completely blended.

2. Add remaining ingredients; stir well until mixture is smooth.

3. Churn-freeze.

A simply delightful taste combination; these two distinctive flavors—cranberry and apple—complement each other most invitingly, but each retains its own identity.

This is a quick and convenient way to use the leftover baked apples in a different dessert without much extra trouble.

Baking Cranapples

If you're going to bake them specially for this ice cream, peel and core the apples. Sprinkle with cranberry juice and ground cardamom (a fine flavor picker-upper for baked apples) and place in a covered baking dish for 45 minutes at 350 degrees. Apples can also be baked with orange or lemon juice.

Aside from all its other many virtues, the apple is considered a terrific natural tranquilizer.

CRANBERRY ICE CREAM

2 c. cranberry sauce   pinch sea salt
3 T. orange juice   2 c. heavy cream
3 T. lemon juice

1. Combine all ingredients and mix until smooth and creamy. Chill.

2. Churn-freeze.

A sharp flavor. Adds a touch of *haute cuisine* to

your Thanksgiving dinner or to any fowl-serving occasion.

The cranberry has become a popular favorite because its tart, good flavor and texture are so adaptable. Choose firm berries of even size that are rich red. Pick over and discard any gnarled or discolored fruit. One quart of cranberries weighs one pound.

When making your cranberry sauce use ¾ cup of honey for every cup of sugar you would normally use.

CUCUMBER ICE CREAM

1 c. cucumber pulp (approx.	⅓ c. honey
1½ large cucumbers)	¼ t. sea salt
2½ c. heavy cream	1 t. kelp

1. Peel cucumbers; slice lengthwise in half, remove seeds, and chop into pieces. Purée in blender or food mill.

2. Combine puréed cucumber, heavy cream, honey, salt, and kelp; blend until smooth.

3. Churn-freeze.

A winsome, natural ice cream that could accompany any main course. Serve on a bed of greens and garnish with cucumber slices.

Equally delicious in summer or winter, this bright green vegetable is a good source of needed nutrition. Like the papaya, it contains the enzyme erepsin, which helps digestion.

We've used kelp as a seasoning to introduce you to this marvelous seaweed that is the richest natural source of food iodine and ocean minerals.

Cucumbers and sour cream have been a longtime favorite in vegetarian restaurants. So, if you like, substitute sour cream for the heavy cream.

Making Mock Sour Cream

Use the real stuff or whip up a marvelous mock sour cream in your blender: Add ¼ cup buttermilk to 1 cup low-fat creamed cottage cheese. Blend at high speed, scraping down the sides until smooth and creamy.

(This "mock" sour cream cannot be used for baking; for everything else it's great.)

If you use the mock sour cream for making the ice cream, add a beaten egg white to the mix.

CURRANT ICE CREAM

1⅓ c. dry currants	2 c. heavy cream
½ c. water	¾ c. honey
½ c. lemon juice	⅛ t. sea salt
1 c. milk	1½ t. vanilla

1. In a saucepan, combine currants, water, and lemon juice. Let the mixture stand at room temperature for 10 minutes, then cook on low heat, stirring occasionally, for 5 minutes. Cool.

2. Combine milk, heavy cream, honey, salt, and vanilla with cooled currant mixture; blend until smooth.

3. Churn-freeze.

A marvelous tasty delight—no chemicals, no preservatives, no flavorings or coloring agents—just natural sweet goodness for you and your family to enjoy.

There are actually two totally different types of currants—fresh and dry. The fresh currant is a small, sweet-tart berry. It is a member of the gooseberry family and there are red, white, and black varieties. The dry currant commonly used in cakes, cookies, and other desserts, with which we are all familiar, is really a dried grape.

If currants are not easily available, this recipe will be just as delicious if you use the ever-popular raisin (seedless, of course).

DATE ICE CREAM

2 eggs	1 c. heavy cream
pinch salt	2 t. vanilla
1½ c. milk	1 c. chopped pitted dates
¼ c. honey	1 t. ginger
½ c. date sugar	

1. Beat eggs and salt until creamy.
2. In top of double boiler, over hot but not boiling water, heat milk until bubbling.
3. Pour hot milk slowly into beaten eggs, stirring vigorously. Mix well and return to top of double boiler. Cook, stirring frequently, until thickened. Cool.
4. Combine cooled mixture with the rest of the ingredients; blend until smooth.
5. Churn-freeze.

A delight to serve—exciting and delicious, sweet and satisfying. For something extraspecial, try soaking the dates in half a cup of orange juice for an hour before chopping.

If you would like to eliminate the honey and use only date sugar (a natural sweetener made from pulverized and crystalized dates), use 1 cup sugar and add ¼ cup milk.

Making a Snowball

Date ice cream makes a divine snowball. Spread some unsweetened, natural shredded coconut on a piece of wax paper. Using a small scoop, roll a ball of ice cream in the shredded coconut and then sprinkle with chopped walnuts. The walnuts are optional but provide a really nice extra touch.

Making Date Sugar

Though it is commonly sold at most health food stores, you can easily make your own date sugar by grinding up pitted, hardened dry dates in a blender. It should be kept in a tightly sealed container and refrigerated. Check occasionally to see that mold does not form.

DATE MOUSSE

1 c. chopped, pitted dates	pinch sea salt
2 c. apple cider	1½ c. heavy cream
2 egg yolks	

1. Combine chopped dates, apple cider, egg yolks, and salt in a blender until thoroughly mixed.
2. Place blended ingredients in top of a double boiler over low heat, stirring frequently, until mixture is thickened. Cool.
3. Add heavy cream.
4. Churn-freeze.

We wanted to give you one recipe without any added sweetener, and this is it! The natural blend of dates and apple cider results in a lovely dessert, unsurpassed for natural sweet flavor. If your sweet tooth is aching, you can add ¼ cup honey or date sugar.

For flavor contrast, top with a dollop of yogurt.

Take a tip from the Middle East and start enjoying this nourishing, easily digested natural fruit as many ways as you can.

EGG SALAD FREEZE

4 slices fresh pineapple
½ c. water
1 env. unflavored gelatin
3 hard-boiled eggs, shelled
¼ c. refined oil
1 t. vanilla

½ t. almond extract
1 c. heavy cream
1 c. sour cream
½ c. raw sugar

1. Cut pineapple into small pieces and soak in water for 10 minutes.

2. Combine gelatin and pineapple with water in saucepan; stir over low heat until gelatin is completely dissolved.

3. Add gelatin mixture to rest of ingredients. Place in an electric blender and blend until smooth and thick. Chill.

4. Churn-freeze.

Most unusual. A new way to use and serve egg salad. Great for those lazy summer days when all you have to do is reach into your freezer. It goes well with any of your favorite greens, surrounded by green pepper rings. Be sure to use fresh eggs.

FIG ICE CREAM

1½ c. milk
½ c. raw sugar
3 egg yolks
½ lb. dried figs

pinch salt
1 T. vanilla
3 egg whites
1 c. heavy cream

1. Heat milk and sugar together in top of double boiler until bubbling.

2. Beat egg yolks until thick; add beaten egg yolks to

the hot milk mixture slowly, beating vigorously as you do. Cook, over low heat, stirring constantly, until thickened. Cool.

3. Grind dried figs and add along with the rest of the ingredients, to the cooled mixture.

4. Churn-freeze.

A taste triumph!

Figs are a wholesome and most nutritious food; however, they are considered a natural laxative and must be eaten in moderation. Therefore, even though you love this dessert, exercise due caution and don't eat the whole quart by yourself.

If you have any trouble grinding the figs in your blender, you may have to add a quarter cup of warm water and stop the blender occasionally so that you can stir the fig mixture around. Try using a chopstick for this purpose; it doesn't get caught in the blade.

Sweet-and-Sour Topping

For an interesting sweet-and-sour effect, top with a sauce made by combining 1 cup of yogurt with ¼–½ cup honey (might be a good idea to try some of those exotic-flavored honeys like Romanian Sandalwood)—adjust the sweetness to your own taste.

FRUIT FANTASY

⅓ c. honey
6 T. crushed pineapple
1 mashed banana
½ c. chopped strawberries
2 oranges, peeled and diced

1 T. lemon juice
1 env. unflavored gelatin
¼ c. cold water
1½ c. heavy cream
½ c. pine nuts

1. Combine honey, pineapple, banana, strawberries, oranges, and lemon juice; blend until smooth.

2. Soften gelatin in ¼ cup water for 5 minutes. Then heat gelatin and water and stir until dissolved.

3. Beat heavy cream until lightly whipped.

4. Add dissolved gelatin, pine nuts, and whipped cream to the fruit mixture.

5. Churn-freeze.

This is our version of a natural tutti-frutti ice cream—a perfect mélange of fruit flavors combined in a dazzling, delicate dessert.

If you would like to make this into a delightful, smooth sherbet, use milk instead of heavy cream. Milk sherbets were discovered by Marco Polo in the thirteenth century while he was traveling to and from the Orient. He brought back with him a recipe that called for milk instead of water; it was used and loved by the Italian aristocracy for hundreds of years. Sherbets remained a luxury food for a long time due to the unavailability of ice. For this reason, early cookbooks contain no mention of them.

Blueberry Topping

Turn this dish into a connoisseur's creation by serving with a fresh blueberry sauce. Combine 1 cup blueberries, 2 tablespoons water, 3 tablespoons honey, and ¼ teaspoon cinnamon in a saucepan and cook for 5 minutes, stirring occasionally. Serve hot or cold over the ice cream.

FRUIT BUTTER ICE CREAM

1 pt. sour cream	10-oz. jar of favorite fruit
1 c. orange juice	butter
2 t. cinnamon	½ c. honey

1. In a blender, combine sour cream, orange juice, cinnamon, fruit butter, and honey. Blend until smooth.

2. Churn-freeze.

A wonderful idea—quick, easy, and delicious. This frozen dessert was made to give anyone the opportunity to turn one of the many fruit butters, which are completely natural, into a simple ice cream. All the butters are made with pure spices, no preservatives, and in some instances a small amount of honey. We used prune-cranberry and got raves from everyone who tested it. Sour cream was included so that the end product would not be too buttery.

Try topping with some crunchy wheat germ, a great source of B complex and E vitamins.

Those of you who are "do-it-yourselfers" may want to experiment with your own fruit butters. You'll find that they're really quite simple to prepare, and when there's extra fruit around this might be a good thing to think about.

GINGER ICE CREAM

1 T. unbleached flour	1½ c. heavy cream
pinch salt	1 egg yolk
½ c. honey	½ c. preserved ginger
1 c. milk	1 t. vanilla

1. Mix flour, salt, honey, milk, and ½ cup of the heavy cream together in top of a double boiler. Cook, over a low flame, stirring often, until well heated and well blended.

2. Beat egg yolk vigorously; add two tablespoons of the hot milk mixture to the yolk and continue beating. Set aside.

3. Chop ginger into fine pieces.

4. Add egg yolk and chopped ginger to the hot honey mixture. Cool.

5. Whip remaining 1 cup of heavy cream lightly. Add whipped cream and vanilla to the cooled mixture.

6. Churn-freeze.

Frozen dessert fanciers will favor this rich, sharply flavored ice cream. Tops off a Chinese dinner just perfectly. Yogurt fans can substitute a cup of yogurt for the cup of milk to bring out an unusual tartness.

You will discover that the spicy taste of the ginger becomes much stronger while on the tongue.

This ice cream should be served within a few hours after freezing. If it is going to be stored for any length of time, you will have to put the mixture through a strainer or a sieve before you add the heavy cream. Also, do not chop the ginger as fine. This will prevent the ginger flavor from becoming too overwhelming.

GRAPE MERINGUE ICE CREAM

6 egg whites
¼ t. sea salt
½ c. raw sugar
2 c. heavy cream

1 c. grape juice
1 c. chopped, pitted grapes
2 t. vanilla

1. Beat egg whites with salt until stiff peaks form.

2. Add sugar to egg whites, a teaspoonful at a time; continue beating until well combined.

3. Lightly whip heavy cream and mix with grape juice and chopped grapes and vanilla.

4. Fold cream mixture into egg whites.

5. Churn-freeze.

Light in texture and taste—good as a snack any time, but especially good after a hearty meal.

There's really no difficulty in handling grapes, even though they are small, if you know what you're doing.

To skin them, plunge in hot water for 2 minutes, then in cold water. The skin will come off easily. To seed them, sterilize a bobby pin with boiling water; push the loop end into the grape at the stalk and pull out the seeds.

No matter how fine grapes may look in the dealer's display case, always check the stem end before purchasing. Look for a green, firm, healthy stem. When the stem looks dry and has started to turn color (black or brown), the grapes have started to age and are losing flavor.

The favorite United States grapes come largely from two areas—from California and Arizona and from the Eastern states. Popular favorites from the East are *Concord* (blue, round grapes, excellent for grape juice, jelly, or table use) and *Niagara* (white grapes, table variety). Those grapes grown in the Eastern regions have skins that separate easily from the pulp but the seeds are hard to remove. Grapes from the West have reverse characteristics and are sweeter. Western notables are *Ribier* (large, black round grapes), *Thompson Seedless* (white, small, olive-shaped grapes), and *Cardinal* (red-purple grapes, heavy and sweet in flavor when fully mature). Which one you choose is up to you; you won't be disappointed in this dessert.

Don't give any thought at all to those extra egg yolks; they won't go to waste. Use for homemade mayonnaise (another one of those dishes that are so easy to make in your blender), fresh custards, and white or hollandaise sauce, or to enhance your favorite soups with a marvelous rich flavor.

GUAVA ICE CREAM

1 c. puréed guavas	1 c. milk
1 T. lime juice	1 c. heavy cream
½ c. guava syrup and concentrate	3 eggs
	¾ c. honey
pinch sea salt	2 t. vanilla

1. Combine puréed guavas with lime juice, guava syrup, and salt. Set aside.

2. Scald milk and cream in top of a double boiler.

3. Beat eggs until light and fluffy and beat in the honey until well combined. Mix with 2 tablespoons of the milk mixture; add to double boiler. Simmer gently over low heat, stirring constantly, until thickened. Remove from heat and cool.

4. Add vanilla to guava purée and mix with cooled milk mixture.

5. Churn-freeze.

Something special, a tart-sweet flavor. For those of you who have not tasted a guava before, it is a pear-shaped tropical fruit resembling the peach in texture. Guavas range in size from that of a cherry to a large pear or apple, and there are several varieties grown in most tropical countries throughout the world.

When puréeing, wash them, cut them in half, skin them, and scoop out the seeds. They are so tender they will quickly cook to the softness you desire.

Should you have trouble locating fresh guavas or any of the other rarer fruits, it is well worth your time and trouble to check the jellies in your favorite health food shop. You will find a large selection of natural jellies; many have only a slight amount of honey and lemon added to them. Instead of the puréed fruit, substitute a 12-ounce jar of natural jelly. Taste for sweetness; it may be that you will have to decrease the amount of honey in our recipe from ¾ cup to ½ or ¼ cup. You'll find the final results just great.

HONEY ICE CREAM

1 env. unflavored gelatin	¾ c. honey
¼ c. water	½ c. nonfat dry milk powder
2 c. milk	2 c. heavy cream
2 eggs	1 T. vanilla
1 T. arrowroot	

1. Soften gelatin in water; stir in milk, eggs, arrowroot, honey, and milk powder and blend until smooth.
2. Transfer mixture to top of a double boiler and cook over low heat, stirring constantly, until mixture thickens. Cool.
3. Add cream and vanilla.
4. Churn-freeze.

A mellifluous mixture that's sheer perfection for even the most demanding honey enthusiasts. For something extraspecial, add ½ cup finely chopped, sun-dried dates before churn-freezing. When combined, these two sweet, natural foods are particularly desirable from a nutritional standpoint and once again prove that natural and delicious are synonymous.

INDIAN PUDDING ICE CREAM

½ c. seedless raisins	2 T. raw or date sugar
2 c. milk	¼ t. cinnamon
⅛ c. cornmeal	¼ t. ginger
1 T. whole-wheat flour	1 T. brewer's yeast
½ c. apple juice or cider	¼ c. unsulfured molasses
pinch sea salt	1 c. heavy cream

1. Chop raisins and cover with warm water to soften. Set aside.

2. Scald milk in top of a double boiler.

3. Make a paste of cornmeal, flour, and apple juice or cider. Add to milk, cover, and cook for 10 minutes. Stir occasionally. Cool.

4. Add remaining ingredients, except cream and raisins, to milk mixture. Blend until smooth.

5. Lightly whip cream and combine with cooled mixture.

6. Remove raisins from water and mix throughout so raisins are evenly distributed.

7. Churn-freeze.

A traditional New England dessert, loved by your great-grandmother, becomes a frozen favorite of your grandchild. Its rich molasses flavor pleases everyone. If you use the dark variety of molasses, you will be getting about fifteen times more iron.

Perfect to serve by itself, or garnished with some apple slices—slice an apple very thin, brush the cut surface with lemon juice to prevent discoloration, and dip in honey.

Custard Sauce Topping

As a special treat, try topping with a rich custard sauce: Beat 2 egg yolks with 2 tablespoons raw sugar and 1 teaspoon arrowroot in top of a double boiler; beat in 1 cup milk. Cook, stirring constantly, over hot, not boiling water for 10 minutes or until custard thickens slightly and coats a spoon. Remove from heat, strain into a small bowl, and stir in 1 teaspoon vanilla.

LEMON CHEESECAKE ICE CREAM

2 c. small-curd cottage
   cheese
¼ c. honey
4 eggs, separated
¼ t. salt

1 t. grated lemon peel
2 T. lemon juice
1 t. vanilla
1 c. unflavored yogurt
⅓ c. honey

1. Combine cottage cheese, ¼ cup honey, egg yolks, salt, lemon peel, lemon juice, vanilla, and yogurt. Blend until smooth.
2. Beat egg whites until soft peaks form, and then gradually add the ⅓ cup of honey. Beat until stiff.
3. Fold egg whites and honey into the cheese mixture, mixing until thoroughly blended.
4. Churn-freeze.

Of all the sinfully sweet desserts in the world, cheesecake ranks supreme. We've turned a universal favorite into a marvelous frozen dessert. You'll enjoy its refreshing tartness. For a delectable touch, top with fresh strawberries or crushed pineapple.

LEMON GRANOLA ICE CREAM

2 c. heavy cream
6 T. fresh lemon juice
¼ c. honey
pinch sea salt

2 T. melted butter
4 oz. granola, finely
   crumbled
¼ c. raw sugar

1. Mix heavy cream, lemon juice, honey, and salt until smooth.
2. In a separate bowl combine melted butter, granola, and raw sugar. Set aside.

3. Churn-freeze cream mixture. Remove from freezer.

4. Add granola mixture, lightly stirring through the cream mixture.

Creamy, crunchy, and piquant. For extra crispiness, add ½ cup of your favorite nuts. (We never get enough nuts and maybe you don't either.) Or use one of the granolas with nuts. The addition of nuts turns this into a "lemony" butter pecan.

If you put this mixture into half-pint paper containers, you can have a quick nutritious breakfast on the run.

LIME ICE

½ c. honey
1¾ c. water
1½ t. gelatin

¼ c. fresh lime juice
grated rind of 1 lime
2 egg whites, stiffly beaten

1. Stir honey and 1½ cups of water; boil for 10 minutes.

2. Soften gelatin in ¼ cup water and add to the boiled honey mixture. Heat until gelatin is completely dissolved. Cool.

3. Add lime juice and rind.

4. Stir in beaten egg whites.

5. Churn-freeze.

Marvelous tart flavor, particularly enjoyable with a sweet wafer. Makes an elegant and easy dessert when served in the center of a fruit cup of honeydew and papaya melon balls and bite-size pieces of pineapple.

When using fresh limes, always select limes that are green (when they turn yellow, they lose flavor and acidity) and heavy for their size. The two most common types of limes are *Key limes,* which are small and round, and *Persian limes,* which resemble lemons in size and shape.

LIME ICE CREAM

¼ c. lime juice
1 T. grated lime rind
1 c. honey
1½ c. milk

3 T. unbleached flour
½ c. water
1½ c. heavy cream

1. Mix lime juice and lime rind together and set aside.

2. Heat honey and milk together and stir until smooth.

3. Blend flour into cold water to make a paste. Add to honey mixture. Cook over low heat until mixture begins to thicken, stirring constantly. Remove from heat. Add lime juice and rind. Chill.

4. Add heavy cream.

5. Churn-freeze.

A tantalizing taste for even the most particular palates. It's silky-smooth, rich, and cream-colored, with a few green spots. Don't say what it is, just serve and ask your guests to tell you. Only a few will be able to guess, but everyone likes it. It's made from the simplest ingredients found in almost everyone's kitchen. We occasionally serve it topped with puréed raspberries.

MANGO ICE CREAM
(Tropical Temptation)

1 c. puréed mango pulp
pinch sea salt
⅛ c. lemon or lime juice
⅔ c. honey

1 c. milk
2 eggs
1 c. heavy cream

1. Combine mango pulp, salt, juice, and 1 tablespoon of the honey together; set aside.

2. Scald milk in the top of a double boiler.

3. Beat eggs with the remaining honey. Mix with 2 tablespoons of the milk and add to double boiler. Simmer gently over low heat, stirring constantly, until mixture thickens. Remove from heat and cool.

4. Whip heavy cream lightly, and combine with mango purée and milk mixture.

5. Churn-freeze.

This is an exotic concoction. The distinctive taste of the tropical mango—rich and sweet but not cloying, a cross among pineapple, peaches, and apricots—makes this an ice cream find. Yes, for every fruit there is a frozen dessert.

The mango is a yellowish green, flattish, oval fruit the size of a large avocado. It is freckled with pink or clear-red spots as it ripens; black areas usually indicate overripeness. It is just perfect when the skin is smooth and it is beginning to change color. A mango that is ready to eat will be "springy" when you gently press the fruit between the palms of your hand. A firm but mature mango will ripen at room temperature in 3 or 4 days. When it's ready to eat, serve at once or else refrigerate in a plastic bag—it will keep only for a few days.

MANGO PINEAPPLE SHERBET

1 c. sliced mangos	½ c. water
1 c. crushed pineapple	1½ c. milk
1 T. lime juice	1 egg white
½ c. honey	

1. Cook mangos in water to cover until soft. Purée with crushed pineapple and lime juice. Cool.

2. Combine honey and water, and heat until a syrupy consistency, stirring occasionally. Cool.

3. Blend fruit purée and honey syrup together with milk.

4. Beat egg white and fold into fruit-honey mixture.

5. Churn-freeze.

A delicate, light flavor—refreshing as a dessert or as a surprise sweet relish with chicken or turkey.

Those of you who are unfamiliar with the delicious mango will find it a wonderful addition to fruit salads; once you try it, you'll enjoy the change of pace this somewhat offbeat fruit adds.

For extraspecial entertaining, take some sliced peaches, orange sections, and fresh berries (or any other fruit combination you like), place in the bottom of your best sherbet glasses, and top with a scoop of sherbet. Sprinkle with shredded coconut.

Grapefruit Topping

Another wonderful touch would be to top with grapefruit: Peel a small pink grapefruit (keep it over a bowl, so you will catch the juice); cut away all the membrane and white part of the rind. Section the grapefruit into the bowl containing the juice. Sprinkle with 3 to 4 tablespoons of raw sugar or honey. Stir and chill.

MAPLE WALNUT ICE CREAM

3 egg yolks	1 t. vanilla
1 T. arrowroot	1½ c. heavy cream
1 c. maple syrup	1 c. chopped walnuts
1 c. milk	
⅛ t. sea salt	

1. Beat egg yolks until lemon-colored and creamy.

2. Combine arrowroot, maple syrup, milk, and salt with beaten egg yolks in top of a double boiler over hot, not boiling water. Cook, stirring constantly, until mixture thickens. Cool.

3. Add vanilla, heavy cream, and chopped walnuts to the cooled mixture.

4. Churn-freeze.

A go-together combination. The unique and delicate flavor of the pure maple syrup is unforgettable. To turn this into a custardy honey walnut ice cream, replace the maple syrup with half a cup of honey. The walnuts, which are rich in unsaturated fatty acids and phosphorous, provide a good source of iron and vitamin B.

For an Ice Cream Cake

This ice cream would be an ideal filling for a jelly-roll of log-type cake. Once rolled, the entire cake could be sprinkled with coconut shreds and chopped walnuts. Almost too pretty to eat!

A word of caution about maple syrup: Once the bottle is open, the syrup will eventually mold. Therefore, after the seal is broken, the syrup should be refrigerated and used within a reasonable length of time.

MILLET-ORANGE-COCONUT SURPRISE

½ c. millet	2 eggs, separated
pinch sea salt	⅓ c. orange juice
2 c. milk	1 c. heavy cream
3 T. grated orange rind	¼ c. shredded coconut
½ c. carob syrup	1 T. vanilla

1. Mix the millet, salt, and ½ cup of the milk in the top of a double boiler.

2. Scald the remaining milk and stir into the millet.

3. Add the orange rind and the carob syrup. Cook, over boiling water, stirring occasionally until the millet is tender. This will take about 15 minutes.

4. Beat the egg yolks lightly and add to the millet mixture, mixing slightly until it thickens. Cool.

5. Add the orange juice, heavy cream, coconut, and vanilla.

6. Beat the egg whites and fold into the mixture.

7. Churn-freeze.

An intriguing taste, proving that sweets need not be just a bunch of empty calories. Tender and chewy, millet is probably one of our most ancient grains, providing lots of nutrition—large amounts of magnesium and potassium as well as some protein. Used for centuries in Asia and many parts of Europe for both humans and animals, only quite recently has it become popular as a breakfast cereal in our country. Nicknamed "poor man's rice," it can be used in place of rice in almost any recipe.

We've come up with two extraordinary toppings for this unusual dessert.

Spicy Fruit Sauce

Add ¼ teaspoon ground allspice, ¼ teaspoon ground cloves, ¼ teaspoon ground cinnamon, 3 tablespoons lemon juice, and ½ cup honey (preferably orange blossom) to your favorite fruit syrup. What zip!

Cream Cheese Smoothie

Whip one 8-ounce package of cream cheese with ⅔ tablespoon honey and the grated peel of one orange. Chill.

MINCEMEAT ICE CREAM

⅓ c. honey   1 lemon
⅛ t. sea salt   1 t. vanilla
2 egg yolks   1 c. cooked mincemeat
1 c. half and half   2 c. heavy cream
2 t. arrowroot

1. Combine honey, salt, and egg yolks in top of a double boiler. Beat until thick and creamy. Add half and half and arrowroot then cook, stirring occasionally, until thickened. Remove from heat. Cool.

2. Squeeze lemon and grate rind.

3. Add lemon juice and rind, vanilla, mincemeat (see below), and heavy cream to the egg mixture; blend until smooth.

4. Churn-freeze.

An ice cream made of sugar, spice, and everything nice. A fruit-filled sensation with a lively tangy flavor that is just right. The mincemeat flavor in the creamy base is so special that you may never make mincemeat pie again.

How to Make Mincemeat

Most important of all, we've managed to produce a true mincemeat flavor without using suet or brandy. We think this recipe is so unusual that you'll want to pass it along to all your friends. For about 3 ½ cups of the tastiest mincemeat, get the following ingredients ready:

1 c. seedless raisins
3 medium-size tart apples,
  cored

½ medium orange
¼ lemon
½ c. apple cider
1 c. date sugar
½ t. sea salt
½ t. cinnamon
½ t. nutmeg
½ t. powdered cloves
½ c. chopped walnuts

Put raisins, apples, orange, and lemon through a food mill or blender. Add cider to puréed fruit and place in a saucepan. Heat to boiling point; cover pan and simmer 10 minutes. Add sugar, salt, cinnamon, nutmeg, and cloves; simmer 15 minutes longer. Remove from heat and add chopped walnuts. Cool.

MINTY FRUIT FREEZE

2 c. sliced mixed fruit
1 c. honey
½ c. water
1 T. lemon juice
½ c. soy milk powder

2 egg yolks
½ c. cold-pressed oil
2 drops oil of peppermint
pinch cinnamon
½ c. heavy cream

1. Purée fruit and honey. Set aside.
2. Make a paste of the water, lemon juice, and soy milk powder. Blend until smooth and thick. Add the egg yolks and stir until thoroughly mixed.
3. Add oil, peppermint oil, and cinnamon.
4. Combine milk mixture with fruit.
5. Lightly beat heavy cream and add to the fruit mixture.
6. Churn-freeze.

A potpourri of perfection. The natural flavors of your favorite fruits combined with the oil of peppermint create this exceptionally delicious ice cream with a stimulating taste. We used a combination of plums, apricots, apples, and berries; it was succulent.

If you use fresh mint, crush or chop about 12 sprigs and combine with the soy milk paste. Heat in the top of a double boiler, then cool and strain before proceeding with step 3 of the recipe.

If you don't have an eyedropper for measuring the oil of peppermint, simply insert a clean toothpick in the bottle and then shake off 2 drops gently into your mixing bowl.

Served in the center of a fruit salad, this makes a lovely, elegant dessert. It's also a luscious accompaniment to freshly baked gingerbread, or you can line the bottom and sides of your favorite bowls with lady fingers, fill with the ice cream, and garnish with leftover berries.

MOLASSES PEANUT BUTTER ICE CREAM

5 T. unsulfured molasses
¼ c. natural peanut butter
1 c. sour cream
pinch sea salt
½ c. water

2 t. vanilla
½ t. cinnamon
½ t. ginger
2 c. heavy cream

1. Combine all ingredients except heavy cream; mix until smooth.
2. Whip heavy cream lightly and fold into molasses mixture.
3. Churn-freeze.

An easy but gala dessert that will surprise and please everyone. The dark delicious flavor of molasses gives this a wide-awake, rich, pungent taste.

A quick energy food, as well as a source of various vitamins B, molasses has been a staple in most kitchens since earliest times. In England, molasses is called treacle. Many people prefer molasses or honey rather than maple syrup on their pancakes.

West Indies and Barbados varieties are the milder, mellow types of molasses.

Making Peanut Butter

There's nothing better than homemade peanut butter, and it's so easy: Put 2 cups natural peanuts in your blender container and blend for one minute. Gradually add ¼ cup peanut oil, a tablespoon at a time—watch carefully and scrape down the sides of the container with a rubber spatula frequently. Add a pinch or two of sea salt if you like your peanut butter salty.

NECTARINE SHERBET

6 fresh ripe nectarines	1¾ c. water
¼ c. orange juice	1 T. grated orange rind
½ c. honey	1 egg white
1 T. lemon juice	1 c. milk

1. Peel and pit nectarines. Purée in a food mill or blender with ¼ cup of the orange juice. Set aside.

2. Combine honey, lemon juice, and water in a small saucepan and heat for 10 minutes. Add the nectarine purée and grated orange rind to the honey mixture and continue cooking, stirring occasionally, for 15 minutes. Cool.

3. Beat egg white lightly and fold into nectarine mixture. Add milk.

4. Churn-freeze.

A kicky, go-with-anything, delicately flavored sherbet you'll be glad you tried—especially when you hear those cries of "seconds, please." So good it will earn a permanent place in your repertoire of dessert recipes.

Nectarines are a distinct member of the peach family and should be selected and cooked accordingly. Mistakenly, they are commonly referred to as a half-breed between peaches and plums. When buying them, avoid hard green or dull-colored fruit, as such coloration indicates that it was picked too soon. You should purchase firm, plump, well-formed fruit with skin that has a blush of red over a yellow or yellow-orange background. A slight softening along the skin seam indicates the fruit's ripeness.

RAW NUT CHEW

2 c. soy milk
1 c. chopped almonds
1 c. chopped pecans
½ c. sunflower seed kernels
¼ c. flaxseed
½ c. honey

¼ c. walnut oil
1 t. vanilla
1 env. gelatin, softened in
  ¼ c. hot water
¼ c. wheat germ

1. Mix all ingredients in blender until smooth.
2. Churn-freeze.

This is a chewy, candylike dessert with nutritional goodness galore. Also excellent when thawed out as a cold Bavarian cream dessert or as a breakfast blend.

The flax plant was said to be found growing wild by the American colonists. In ancient times flaxseeds were munched between courses. You can see that they have been with us for a long time, but this Nut Chew won't because its taste is unique and satisfying.

ORANGE-DATE DIVINE

⅔ c. honey
⅓ c. date sugar
¼ c. water
1 c. orange juice
2 egg yolks
½ c. half and half

1 t. grated orange rind
½ c. heavy cream
¼ c. chopped, pitted dates
1 c. unsweetened, natural
    shredded coconut

1. Boil honey, sugar, and water together for 5 minutes. Add orange juice.

2. Beat egg yolks and half and half together. Add to honey mixture with grated orange rind. Chill.

3. Whip heavy cream lightly; fold into honey mixture along with the chopped dates and shredded coconut.

4. Churn-freeze.

This one is an ambrosia-type dessert fit for the gods. The blend of coconut and dates is distinct, but no special flavor is overwhelming—however, the individual elements can be perceived.

We like it with a topping of chopped dates and nuts that have been dipped in ½ cup orange juice for moisture.

ORANGE FREEZE

1 c. water
½ c. raw sugar
3 c. orange juice

½ t. orange rind
½ t. lemon rind

1. In a small saucepan combine water and sugar, and cook until syrup comes to a boil. Cool.

2. Mix cooled sugar syrup with remaining ingredients.

3. Churn-freeze.

Tastes just like it sounds! This is a fine way to use up those oranges that are beginning to get soft. For a nice flavor, chop some of the orange pulp finely and add it to the juice. For a sparkling variation, add one tablespoon of mint leaves to the cooled sugar syrup before combining it with the orange juice. Strain the mixture before churn-freezing.

When selecting oranges, choose heavy fruit, not paying too much attention to color—many fruits are sprayed to obtain that rich orange hue. Avoid fruit with soft or dark spots.

ORANGE YOGURT CRUNCH

1 c. orange juice	1½ c. heavy cream
3 T. grated orange rind	1 T. lemon juice
⅔ c. carob syrup	1 t. vanilla
pinch sea salt	1 t. almond extract
1½ c. yogurt	½ c. chopped, unsalted soy
2 egg whites	nuts

1. Combine orange juice, orange rind, carob syrup, salt, and yogurt; blend until smooth.

2. Beat egg whites until stiff and fold into yogurt mixture.

3. Add heavy cream, lemon juice, vanilla, almond extract, and soy nuts.

4. Churn-freeze.

A delectable dessert that has a touch of freezer magic. It's especially good if you use yogurt made at home (half the cost of commercial brands, more delicious, and far superior). We prefer the following method.

Homemade Yogurt

Bring 1 quart of milk to a boil, then allow it to cool until you can put your finger in and keep it there for about 10 seconds—it feels warm but not hot (usually 150 degrees, but no more). For a starter, put two or three tablespoons of plain yogurt in a large Pyrex bowl, and beat well with a whisk. Add ½ cup of the milk, a spoonful at a time, beating well after each addition, then the rest of the milk all at once, beating constantly. Cover the bowl tightly with a plastic wrap and secure with toweling and a small cotton blanket. Leave for 8 to 10 hours in a warm place, at 85° to 95°, then refrigerate.

The finished product will be absolutely smooth and mild-flavored. If it has a strong, sour taste, it was left in the heat too long. Too much heat will also produce a tough or curdled texture.

Always save some to use as a starter for your next batch. Many people prefer a yogurt maker or culturizer; they are easily available and not too expensive. No matter what you do, make your own.

Homemade Sour Cream

Now that you're a yogurt expert, you may want to go all the way and try your hand at sour cream. It's really simple, once you've done the yogurt.

All you have to do is place 1 pint of light sweet cream in a clean jar, add 2 tablespoons of your delicious yogurt, mix, and set in a warm place overnight. Then refrigerate. Of course, you can also use cultured buttermilk instead of yogurt as the starter. Buttermilk is generally used.

PAPAYA CRUNCH DELIGHT

2 c. papaya purée
⅓ c. lemon juice
⅓ c. orange juice
⅓ c. papaya juice
1 T. grated orange and
   lemon rind

pinch sea salt
½ c. honey
1 c. goat's milk
1 c. goat's heavy cream
1 c. crumbled natural
   cereal

1. Combine papaya purée, juices, rind, salt, honey, and goat's milk in blender. Blend until smooth and creamy. Cool.

2. Whip cream lightly. Fold cream into papaya mixture.

3. Add the natural cereal, mixing lightly throughout.

4. Churn-freeze.

Make it once and you'll have to make it again and again. We think you will agree that this is a new and fabulous way to serve this exotic melon.

Papayas are ready to eat when the green rind has turned yellow; if you select one that's started to color and has speckled yellow over 35 percent or more, of the fruit, you will have a melon that will ripen completely in 2 or 3 days at room temperature. A ripe papaya can be stored in the refrigerator for 1 or 2 days.

Now that you've been introduced to papaya, eat it often. It is sometimes called the "wonder" fruit since it possesses such extraordinarily high nutritive qualities. Papaya is richer in vitamins than almost any other fruit known. It also contains a ferment known as papain, which has a pronounced salutory effect upon the entire digestive system. When eaten raw, the melon is mildly sweet with a slight musky tang.

Several old established companies are now marketing "natural cereals," or you may choose a granola.

PAPAYA-ORANGE-GRAPEFRUIT SHERBET

1 c. sliced papaya
1 c. shredded orange and
    grapefruit pulp
⅓ c. orange juice
½ c. raw sugar

1 t. cinnamon
½ t. dried orange peel
pinch sea salt
2 egg whites
1 c. light cream

1. Combine papaya slices, orange and grapefruit pulp, orange juice, raw sugar, cinnamon, and dried orange peel.
2. Add salt to egg whites and beat until stiff. Fold into fruit mixture.
3. Blend in cream.
4. Churn-freeze.

Cool, refreshing, and nutritious, too. Serve with fresh orange slices or drained, canned mandarin orange and mint sprays.

Grapefruit, popular for breakfast, lunch, and dinner, or any time of day at all, gives this sherbet a special tang. In combination with other fruits the grapefruit provides a flavor picker-upper. Grapefruit, like most other fruits, is low in sodium and fat and high in vitamin C. A grapefruit half contains almost 50 percent of the ascorbic acid you should be getting every day.

PEACH BUTTERMILK ICE CREAM

1 env. unflavored gelatin
¼ c. cold water
1½ c. buttermilk
⅔ c. honey
2 egg yolks
pinch sea salt

1 c. finely diced fresh
    peaches
½ t. ground cloves
1 T. honey
1 t. vanilla
¼ t. almond extract
1 c. heavy cream

1. Soften gelatin in water.

2. Place buttermilk and honey in top of a double boiler; cook until thoroughly blended.

3. Beat egg yolks with salt and combine with 2 tablespoons of the buttermilk mixture.

4. Stir beaten eggs into the hot milk mixture and continue cooking, stirring constantly, until smooth and creamy.

5. Add softened gelatin and cook milk mixture for an additional 5 minutes. Cool.

6. Purée peaches with 1 tablespoon of honey and ground cloves.

7. Combine cooled buttermilk mixture with vanilla, almond extract, and heavy cream.

8. Add pouréed peaches.

9. Churn-freeze.

The perfect flavor (tangy and quite tasty) but oh, so delicate! A really carefree summertime dessert that could easily be the start of an ice cream renaissance. Most favorite cookbooks include an ice cream freezer in its list of household needs. With results like this, you can see why. So, better start giving ice cream freezers as that really different shower gift—with a copy of this book, of course.

Peaches are so abundant in the United States and generally have such an excellent flavor that we could easily regard them as our own national fruit. They are the third most important fruit crop in this country. If the blush on the skin of a peach is too red, the fruit inside will be dull and brown, so don't be fooled into thinking it's rosy rich.

PEACHY CARROT ICE CREAM

1 c. sliced carrots	¼ t. mace
1 c. sliced peaches	¼ t. cinnamon
1 c. apple juice	2 egg whites
½ c. honey	2 T. dry milk
pinch sea salt	1 c. heavy cream

1. Purée carrots and peaches with apple juice.

2. Combine carrot purée with honey, salt, mace, cinnamon, egg whites, and dry milk; blend until smooth.

3. Whip heavy cream lightly and add to carrot mixture.

4. Churn-freeze.

The carrots enhance the peach flavor without completely losing their character. This taste treat can be served as a dessert or as a lively accompaniment to roast duck or pork.

Luckily for peach lovers, the peach season is a long and plentiful one—peaches are available from May through October and fresh peaches are exported from South America in January through April. The peach originated as a wild fruit in China, and in the Orient the peach tree was considered a symbol of long life, so much so that porcelain plates with peach blossoms painted on them were given as birthday gifts. Today, many naturalists consider peaches so vital to good health that they feel eating large amounts of peaches while they are in season benefits the body year around.

The most common varieties of peaches are *Clingstone* and *Freestone* and in selecting look for plump, smooth-skin, well-filled-out fruit. Peaches should not be washed before storing in the refrigerator.

Carrots are one of those rare vegetables that retain their most important nutrients reasonably well outside of the refrigerator, provided they are kept cool and moist enough to prevent withering.

PEANUT BUTTER ICE CREAM

2 eggs	1 c. natural peanut butter
1 c. milk	2 t. vanilla
¾ c. honey	3 c. light cream
2 T. arrowroot	1 c. chopped, unsalted
¼ t. salt	roasted peanuts

1. Beat eggs in a bowl with a wire whisk. Set aside.

2. In top of double boiler, combine milk, honey, arrowroot, and salt, mixing thoroughly.

3. Cook mixture over hot water, stirring constantly, until mixture is slightly thickened.

4. Stir a few tablespoons of the hot milk mixture into beaten eggs.

5. Return milk-egg mixture to double boiler and cook, stirring constantly, for 2 minutes. Remove from heat.

6. Combine and blend hot mixture with the peanut butter. Cool.

7. Add vanilla and light cream to the peanut butter mixture.

8. Churn-freeze.

9. Add nuts, mixing lightly throughout.

A delicious, wholesome mix—crisp and crunchy—perfect. A particular favorite with youngsters. Grown-ups may prefer sesame seeds instead of peanuts.

Raw nuts should not be used, because they are far too bland.

Natural peanut butter must always be thoroughly mixed, since it does not contain chemicals that make many commercial butters so smooth.

PEAR SHERBET

1 lb. ripe Bartlett pears	1 t. nutmeg
2 T. lemon juice	½ c. honey
1 t. cinnamon	½ c. water
2 T. chopped, preserved ginger	2 c. light cream

1. Peel, core, and dice pears. Combine pears with lemon juice, cinnamon, ginger, nutmeg, honey, and water in a medium saucepan and cook over low heat until pears are tender, but not mushy. Remove from heat and blend until smooth. Cool.

2. Add light cream to the cooled pears; mix well.

3. Churn-freeze.

A pungent full-flavored sherbet—very spicy and very special. The rich, juicy, sweet Bartletts (known as the all-purpose pear) and the honey, ginger, cinnamon, nutmeg, and lemon are a really satisfying combination.

Never store pears in the refrigerator before they are ripe, because they then have a tendency to rot and flavor will not reach its peak.

Preserved ginger in syrup is available in most specialty food stores. It's always in stock at Oriental shops.

PINE NUT ICE CREAM

¾ c. goat's milk	¼ c. lemon juice
1 T. vanilla	1 egg
1 T. unbleached flour	1½ c. goat's heavy cream
⅛ t. sea salt	1 c. pine nuts (pignolias)
⅔ c. honey	

1. In the top of a double boiler, heat milk and vanilla until bubbling.

2. Add flour and salt to the hot mixture. Cook, stirring frequently, until mixture is slightly thickened.

3. Stir honey and lemon juice into the thickened milk mixture.

4. Beat egg lightly with 2 tablespoons of the hot milk mixture. Add the beaten egg to the hot milk and cook over low, not boiling, heat for 5 minutes. Cool.

5. Whip cream lightly; fold into cooled milk mixture.

6. Add pine nuts; mixing lightly throughout the mixture.

7. Churn-freeze.

You can't help liking this ice cream, which is certain to become an all-time favorite. The crunch and delicate flavor of the pine nuts are exceptional. Enjoy this ice cream *au naturel* or add a dab of your favorite whipped cream and loads of additional nuts.

Seeds and nuts (which are really seeds in a shell) are nature's own "core of life"; and we never get enough of them. Pine nuts grow in the wild and are really an excellent food because they are completely natural, never having been subjected to harmful poison sprays or chemical fertilizers.

PINEAPPLE AMBROSIA

½ c. honey
1 egg
1 c. heavy cream
¾ c. light cream
1 t. vanilla
½ t. lemon juice

pinch sea salt
½ c. unsweetened, natural shredded coconut
1 c. crushed pineapple, drained

1. Combine honey and egg together until well blended.

2. Add balance of ingredients to the honey-egg mixture; blend until smooth.

3. Churn-freeze.

A perfect balance of sweetness. This dessert is appealing and impressive but quite easy to make—just one mix in your favorite bowl and into the freezer can!

The dictionary says ambrosia was the food of the Greek and Roman gods, something extremely pleasing to taste, as well as a dessert of fruit topped with shredded coconut. We've made it simple for you to luxuriate in it all.

PINEAPPLE-BANANA-ORANGE SORBET

½ c. honey
1 c. crushed pineapple, drained
½ c. orange pulp
3 medium bananas

3 T. orange juice
1 T. lemon juice
2 egg whites
pinch salt

1. Combine honey, crushed pineapple (which has been thoroughly drained), and orange pulp and chill for 1 hour.

2. Mash bananas until finely puréed, or use a blender, sieve, or food mill.

3. Stir orange juice and lemon juice with puréed bananas; add to the chilled honey mixture. Blend until smooth.

4. Beat egg whites with salt until stiff. Fold into fruit mixture.

5. Churn-freeze.

A particularly frosty, mellow-tasting dessert with a predominant banana flavor. Sorbet is merely another name for an ice made with juice of several fruits and the pulp of one of them.

The banana pulp and egg whites will prevent this dessert from melting as quickly as most ices usually do.

However, eat it fast—once everyone trys it, there won't be any left!

PINEAPPLE BUTTERMILK SHERBET

1 env. unflavored gelatin
½ c. water
½ c. honey
1 T. lemon rind
1 T. orange rind

½ c. unsweetened pineapple juice
pinch sea salt
2 c. buttermilk

1. Soften gelatin in water for 5 minutes.
2. Combine honey with gelatin in top of a double boiler and cook over hot water, stirring constantly, for about 5 minutes or until gelatin is completely dissolved. Cool.
3. Add remaining ingredients and mix until smooth.
4. Churn-freeze.

A tangy, tasteful delight that's so good for you and your family. One cup of buttermilk is chock full of nutritional goodness. Remember, to keep it fresh, refrigerate buttermilk as soon as you get home from the store. Also, always check the taste before using.

Did you know that buttermilk is practically fat-free, very low in calories, and especially recommended for many weight-reducing diets?

For a great combination, serve topped with natural-pack pineapple, crushed or sliced. If you wish a more distinctive taste, a stronger flavored juice can be substituted for the pineapple juice.

PINEAPPLE RICE ICE CREAM

1 c. milk	1 T. vanilla
1 c. half and half	½ t. almond extract
¼ c. rice cereal	1 t. cinnamon
¾ c. honey	1 c. heavy cream
1 c. natural-pack crushed pineapple	

1. In a medium saucepan, heat milk and half and half; slowly stir in rice cereal. Cook, while stirring, for 10 minutes. Remove from heat.

2. Stir honey into hot mixture. Cool.

3. Place pineapple in blender or press through a fine sieve or strainer to crush more finely.

4. Add pineapple, vanilla, almond extract, and cinnamon to cooled rice mixture; blend until smooth.

5. Add heavy cream.

6. Churn-freeze.

We used a toasted stone-ground brown rice cereal as a base and added some pineapple to give a tasty tan dessert. Very mild and delicious. Once you try the rice cream, you'll find that your children will also love rice as a breakfast cereal.

There are many thousands of varieties of rice. It has been grown since ancient times, and today probably half the people on earth use it as a means of subsistence. Small wonder, as it has high protein, vitamins, and minerals.

If you have leftover cooked rice and would like to make ice cream with it, substitute the cooked rice in the same quantity as the rice cereal and proceed with step 1, heating only for 5 minutes. Before proceeding with step 2, stir the rice mixture. You might also want to add some finely chopped nuts to the mix before freezing; this will add to the taste.

For something extraspecial try this ice cream with a tart 'n tasty fruit sauce.

PLUM SHORTCAKE

1 c. milk	1 c. fresh plum purée
1 c. heavy cream	1 c. honey
3 egg yolks	½ t. cinnamon
1 c. crumbled soya cookies	2 t. vanilla

1. In top of a double boiler, scald milk and cream.

2. Beat egg yolks until light and fluffy. Mix with 2 tablespoons of the milk mixture; add to double boiler. Simmer gently over low heat, stirring constantly, until thickened. Remove from heat and cool.

3. Add crumbled cookies, plum purée, honey, cinnamon, and vanilla to cooled milk mixture. Mix well.

4. Churn-freeze.

Politically speaking, "plums" are something special. Dessert-wise, you'll find this to be plum-perfection. There are hundreds of varieties of plums grown. Try a few of them and find your own specific favorite.

To peel your plums before puréeing, dip them in boiling water briefly or until the skin bursts. Then peel as you would a tomato. Don't forget that plums turn from ripe to overripe faster than almost any other fruit. Also, they should be refrigerated and stored in a plastic bag or other moisture-proof container to prevent them from shriveling. They are extra good topped with a dab of yogurt. Another delicious topping can be made by adding crushed meringue shells to whipped heavy cream.

Depending on the natural sweetness of the plums that you use, adjust the amount of honey—it may turn out that ½ cup will be just right. Also, when puréeing the plums, try adding a pinch of sea salt.

POMEGRANATE ICE

1 c. raw sugar	1 T. lemon juice
1½ c. water	6 T. orange juice and pulp
4 ripe pomegranates	

1. Combine sugar and water; bring to a boil and cook 5 minutes. Leave in saucepan.
2. Cut pomegranates in half. Remove seeds and pulp; place in a juicer or put through a potato masher.
3. Add strained pomegranates and all other ingredients to the sugar syrup. Simmer, stirring occasionally, for about 15 minutes. Cool.
4. Churn-freeze.

A scrumptious, colorful dessert. Its sweet, dry winy taste is so unusual that most people will not be able to identify this purple surprise. Don't tell them what it is until after they've eaten it. Pomegranate is an autumn-winter fruit with a hard yellow-orange rind. It is also the base for grenadine syrup.

We were delighted to use our juicer-extractor for this dessert. Then we discovered pomegranate juice in the specialty and health food stores. If you buy the juice, check the label to see if any of the above ingredients have already been added. If so, adjust accordingly. Use about 1 ½ cups.

Whether you try the fresh fruit or the juice, the important thing is to try this recipe—it should not be missed. It's the nearest you'll come to iced wine.

PRUNE LEMON PERFECTION

1½ c. prunes	⅛ t. sea salt
1 t. grated lemon rind	¾ c. honey
½ c. lemon juice	½ c. heavy cream
2 eggs	1½ c. milk

1. In a saucepan, soak prunes in 1 cup hot water for 10 minutes. Remove pits. Cook prunes in water till soft. Drain prunes. (Save the water—it is vitamin filled.)

2. Purée prunes in a blender or food mill with rind and lemon juice.

3. Beat eggs lightly and mix with salt, honey, heavy cream, and milk.

4. Add puréed prunes to the egg mixture; blend until smooth.

5. Churn-freeze.

An excellent sweet 'n sour taste. The lemon juice emphasizes the prune flavor and cuts the sweetness. For a delightful variation, use 1 cup prunes and ½ cup apricots.

Do you know that prunes are rich in vitamins A, B, B_2 and niacin, as well as calcium and potassium? Also, they provide quick energy at a mere 18 calories or so a prune.

Get the prunes ready by cooking them the night before and then remove the pits. After that, it's all downhill.

Put the prune water in a covered jar with a few drops of fresh lemon juice. Keep it in the refrigerator; it's so good for you and so refreshing when you are really thirsty.

PUMPKIN NUT ICE CREAM

1 c. cooked, puréed pumpkin	½ t. cinnamon
3 egg yolks	½ t. nutmeg
½ c. honey	½ t. ginger
pinch salt	2 c. heavy cream
	½ c. chopped nuts

1. Purée pumpkin according to instructions below.

2. Beat egg yolks until thick and creamy.

3. Combine puréed pumpkin, egg yolks, honey, salt, cinnamon, nutmeg, and ginger in top of a double boiler over hot, not boiling, water. Cook, stirring occasionally, until mixture is well blended and slightly thickened. Cool.

4. Add nuts and heavy cream to the cooled pumpkin mixture.

5. Churn-freeze.

Happy Thanksgiving! And it will be if you end your holiday dinner with this rich and wonderfully delicious crunchy treat. You can be sure that no one will complain about the missing pumpkin pie.

There are two ways to purée pumpkin: (1) Wash the pumpkin well; cut it in half, and scrape out the seeds (dry and save them). Cut the halves into small pieces about 2" square; place in a large pot and add enough water to cover the bottom of the pot. Cook, stirring often, until very tender and drain. Put the cooked pulp through a strainer or food mill until fine. (2) Proceed as above and after the pumpkin is halved, place halves on a pan with the shell side up; bake in a 325° oven until tender (usually about 1 hour). Scrape out pulp and mash well, or put through a strainer or food mill.

Place the dried seeds on a cookie sheet and bake them in the oven for about 20 minutes. Now's the time to introduce your family to the seed-munching habit—a great way to get all the necessary elements you need, especially zinc. Remember, chopped pumpkin seeds can also be used to replace nuts in any recipe.

QUINCE ICE CREAM

4 medium-size quinces	1 egg
½ lemon	½ T. unbleached flour
½ orange	1 c. honey
½ c. orange juice	pinch sea salt
1 T. fortified nonfat dry milk	1 c. half and half
1 c. milk	½ c. heavy cream
	1 T. vanilla

1. Peel quinces; cut into eighths. Peel and seed lemon and orange. Place all fruit in a small saucepan with ½ cup orange juice and cook until tender. Stir it frequently from the bottom, as it is apt to stick. It may be necessary to add a little additional water if the mixture becomes too thick. Purée in a food mill or blender. Set aside to cool.

2. Add dry milk to one cup milk and bring to a boil in top of a double boiler.

3. Beat egg and make a paste with flour, honey, and salt. Slowly add hot milk to the egg mixture, continuing to beat as you add the milk. Return to top of double boiler and cook for 15 minutes, stirring occasionally. Cool.

4. Add half and half, heavy cream, vanilla, and quince purée to the cooled egg mixture.

5. Churn-freeze.

An intriguing taste experience. This golden fruit, which resembles a yellow apple, is primarily used for making jelly or jam. When it is eaten raw, the taste is quite astringent; this accounts for its popularity in making preserves. Therefore, this recipe may be quite a conversation piece—and will surely create a host of new quince fans.

. For added nutrition we've included a tablespoon of dry skim milk in the mix; lots of good, good vitamins and no loss of flavor.

Low-Calorie Topping

If you want a low-calorie topping that can be served immediately after it's made, try the following: Take ½ cup dry milk powder, ½ cup ice water, and 2 table-spoons lemon juice; blend milk and water in a bowl, whipping 3 to 4 minutes until soft peaks form. Add lemon juice and continue to beat 3 to 4 minutes more. Spoon over ice cream.

RHUBARB SHERBET

1 c. honey
1 c. water
1¼ c. cooked rhubarb
    purée

1 T. lemon juice
4 egg whites

1. Combine honey and water in top of a double boiler and head for 5 minutes, stirring occasionally. Cool.

2. Add puréed rhubarb and lemon juice to the cooled honey syrup.

3. Beat egg whites lightly and fold into rhubarb mixture.

4. Churn-freeze.

A luscious, rosy sherbet. If you like rhubarb, you will certainly love this dessert. It is sweet and sour, slightly on the tart side. It can usually be eaten right from the freezer, as it doesn't harden as solidly as some of the others.

The rhubarb plant can be classified as an herb; however, for cooking purposes, the piquant, sour, juicy flavor of its stalks render it a fruit. Rhubarb must always be stewed with a small amount of sweetener, and the leaves and ends of the stems must be removed and discarded. Though the stems are delicious, rhubarb leaves should *not* be eaten as their large quantities of oxalic acid make them poisonous.

Rhubarb plants require little attention, and without replanting a new crop keeps growing year after year. If allowed to flower, it is beautiful and is often used as a perennial border in gardens.

RHUBARB STRAWBERRY CREME

1 c. stewed rhubarb	pinch sea salt
1 c. sliced strawberries	½ t. cinnamon
½ c. orange juice	1½ c. heavy cream
⅔ c. honey	

1. Purée rhubarb, strawberries, and orange juice in a food mill or blender.
2. Combine with other ingredients; mixing well.
3. Churn-freeze.

These two fruits produce a frozen dessert with an incomparably fine flavor. You'll find the agreeably pungent flavor of rhubarb combined with the natural sweet taste of strawberries to be particularly satisfying and refreshing.

Rhubarb is especially good when mixed with other fruits. Referred to as a "spring tonic," it is now available all year around—thanks to hothouse cultivation—and can always be found in the frozen food sections of any supermarket. The leaves, which should not be eaten, make a marvelous cleaner for discolored aluminum pots and pans.

Since strawberries are also available year around, either fresh or frozen, this can become one of your favorite standard recipes.

ROQUEFORT-RICOTTA APPLE DELIGHT

6 oz. Roquefort cheese	3 eggs, separated
4 oz. ricotta cheese	1 T. honey
pinch sea salt	1 T. lemon juice
2 c. light cream	½ t. nutmeg
2 T. unbleached flour	1 t. vanilla
¼ c. apple juice	

1. Crumble Roquefort cheese and combine with ricotta cheese, salt, and 1 cup of light cream in the top of a double boiler. Cook, stirring occasionally, for 10 minutes.

2. Make a paste of the flour and apple juice. Add to the Roquefort mixture.

3. Beat egg yolks individually until light and fluffy. Add to the Roquefort mixture one at a time, beating the entire mixture well after each addition. Remove from heat. Cool.

4. Add honey, lemon juice, and nutmeg.

5. Beat egg whites and fold into Roquefort mixture.

6. Add the other cup of light cream and vanilla.

7. Churn-freeze.

Fruit and cheese have long been known for their natural affinity for each other. Many successful hosts and hostesses consider them the perfect finale for any occasion.

With this dessert, you are about to experience an exciting taste. Beloved by gourmets since the first century A.D., Roquefort has its own special, strong flavor. We've taken it one step further and refined it by blending with neutral ricotta cheese and light cream to produce a pleasing, frozen dessert.

Made from ewe's-milk (never cow's) from the village of Roquefort in Aveyron in south-central France, genuine Roquefort cheese always carries a Red Sheep Seal on its foil wrapping.

Roquefort continues to gain sharpness during storage, and this dessert should be kept no longer than a week.

SENEGALESE SURPRISE

¼ c. butter	2 apples, peeled and chopped
2 medium onions, coarsely chopped	1 c. cooked chicken, diced
3 stalks celery, finely chopped	1½ c. chicken broth
2 T. whole-wheat flour	1 bay leaf
1 T. curry powder	1 c. light cream

1. Melt the butter in a skillet; add the onions and celery. Cook until the vegetables are translucent.

2. Add the flour and curry powder and continue cooking, stirring for 5 minutes.

3. Place the mixture in an electric blender; add the apples, chicken, and 1 cup of the chicken broth. Blend until smooth, but do not purée.

4. Transfer the mixture to a saucepan and add the remaining broth and the bay leaf. Cook about 10 minutes. Remove the bay leaf. Cool.

5. Stir in the light cream.

6. Churn-freeze.

An excitingly different taste makes this classic soup an unusual frozen treat for jaded palates. Would be glorious served in the center of a Waldorf salad on your favorite greens as a unique appetizer-salad course. Just as good when made with leftover turkey.

This frozen discovery was the result of having a cold Senegalese soup at one of New York's finest hotel restaurants, the Algonquin. You can make an ice cream out of many interesting cold soups. Never use more than 2 tablespoons of flour for a quart of ice cream, and always cut the ingredients much finer than you would for soup so that they do not clog the dasher.

SOUR CREAM FRUIT SHERBET

1 c. sour cream	1 egg
1 c. milk	4 t. fruit concentrate
1½ c. raw sugar	¼ c. lemon juice

1. Place all ingredients in a blender and blend until smooth and creamy. Chill.
2. Churn-freeze.

A melt-in-your mouth, creamy dessert requiring little time and effort. You'll find that sour-cream-base frozen desserts emphasize any fruit's tartness. Also, they stay softer in the freezer and can be used almost at once when guests drop in.

A dash of imagination about fruit toppings to perk up its flavor will turn this into a glamorous dessert. You will also have a chance to use the various purée food concentrates now available in many flavors in a creative and flexible way.

STRAWBERRY-BANANA-WALNUT ICE CREAM
(Serendipity Supreme)

1 c. milk	2 ripe, medium bananas
2 eggs	3 T. orange juice
⅔ c. honey	1 T. lemon juice
2 t. vanilla	1 c. heavy cream
1 c. sliced strawberries	½ c. chopped walnuts

1. Blend all ingredients, except heavy cream and walnuts, until smooth.

2. Whip cream lightly and combine with fruit mixture.

3. Churn-freeze.

4. After taking dasher out of the freezing can, pour walnuts on top of the mixture and slowly mix them throughout with a thin spatula.

"Serendipity," according to the dictionary, is a word coined by Horace Walpole about 1754 meaning "an apparent aptitude for making fortunate discoveries accidentally." All in all, a perfect description of our reaction to this marvelous medley of interesting tastes.

Bananas are just right when the skin darkens and is flecked with brown. Usually a "must" in the infant's diet, adults too need this excellent source of vitamins A, B, and G, riboflavin, and important minerals (potassium, sodium, and chlorine).

The strawberry is a marvelous member of any home garden since it is so easily grown. It does well in any soil that produces good vegetables, and there are innumerable varieties to choose from. If you want to be the first to enjoy your strawberries, protect the patch with fine wire fencing; otherwise, you will be sharing them with small friends of the field.

STRAWBERRY SOUR CREAM ICE CREAM

1 qt. fresh strawberries   ¾ c. honey
½ c. water   2 c. sour cream

1. Wash, hull, and slice strawberries in half.

2. Combine strawberries, water, and ¼ cup of the honey in a saucepan. Cook, covered, over low heat, stirring occasionally, until strawberries soften but are not mushy. Cool.

3. Blend strawberries, remaining ½ cup of honey, and sour cream until smooth.

4. Churn-freeze.

Luscious is the word for this pink, smooth-tasting culinary marvel. Thanks to freezing, strawberries can now be had at any time of the year, so if you like, substitute a 20-ounce package of thawed frozen strawberries. You'll also find that other berries taste just as yummy, so use any of your favorites. You may easily become a sour cream expert.

Before purchasing sour cream, make sure that the container lid is on tight, and check for appearance and aroma. There should be no smell and it should be pure white. The freshest sour cream will not have a layer of moisture (whey) on top, but if it is there you can still produce a normal consistency by merely mixing. Always keep the container in the coldest part of your refrigerator but do not freeze.

Strawberry ice cream is usually made with heavy sweet cream. In using sour cream the butter taste is eliminated and the natural flavor of the strawberry is brought out.

SWEET POTATO ICE CREAM

2 c. sweet potato purée	½ c. maple syrup
2 eggs	½ c. orange juice
2 t. nutmeg	1 T. grated orange rind
pinch allspice	2 c. heavy cream

1. Combine all ingredients in blender and mix until smooth.

2. Churn-freeze.

Easy does it! Just one mix in the blender and you can turn out an innovative surprise full of an unusual natural sweetness. The orange juice and maple syrup blend in a special way to enhance that sweet potato flavor. Yams can be substituted; they are a good alternate. But we just couldn't substitute the word "yam" for potato in the title. Either, however, makes a unique Thanksgiving, Christmas, or any winter day fun-time dish.

Sweet potatoes may be peeled and cooked in boiling water to cover until they are done, or they may be cooked in their jackets. They are a highly nutritious, delicious food and one of the oldest cultivated vegetables in America.

The sweet potato and yam plants are not related to each other, nor to the white potato. However, the resemblance among their edible roots is close enough so that they may be treated as one class of vegetable. There are many varieties of the sweet potato and the yam; they are usually yellow or orange and moderate in size (4 to 12 ounces). The chief distinction between the two is that the sweet potato is long, narrow, and tapering while the yam is thicker and blunt and is also much more moist and is a darker color. Generally, the two are interchangeable, but the drier, firmer flesh of the sweet potato makes it more adaptable to combinations.

TANGERINE SHERBET

1 env. unflavored gelatin	1 c. shredded tangerine pulp
½ c. water	2 T. tangerine rind
¾ c. raw sugar	pinch allspice
1 c. fresh tangerine juice	2 c. buttermilk

1. In the top of a double boiler, sprinkle gelatin over cold water to soften.
2. Add sugar and cook, stirring constantly, until gelatin is completely dissolved.
3. Stir in tangerine juice, pulp, rind, allspice, and buttermilk. Cool.
4. Churn-freeze.

Easy to make—beginners or experienced cooks will produce a tangy, cool dessert with this velvety mixture. A special surprise for the whole family during the Christmas holiday season, the peak period of availability for this medium-size, deep-orange citrus. Beware of puffy skins, which indicate overripeness.

Most people do not recognize the fruit flavor of this sherbet, as the tangerine has such a light taste. That's why we were so pleased to find that only a pinch of allspice brought it to perfection.

TEA AND HONEY ICE CREAM

1 c. milk	½ c. honey
1 c. half and half	2 t. grated orange rind
2 t. peppermint leaves	2 c. heavy cream
3 teabags	3 egg whites
3 egg yolks	

1. Heat milk, half and half, and peppermint leaves in the top of a double boiler.

2. Steep tea bags in hot milk for 5 minutes.

3. Remove tea bags and strain milk mixture, returning it to the top of the double boiler.

4. Beat egg yolks with honey until well combined. Mix with 2 tablespoons of the milk mixture; add to the double boiler. Simmer gently over low heat, stirring constantly, until thickened. Cool.

5. Stir in grated orange rind and heavy cream.

6. Beat egg whites until fluffy and fold into tea mixture.

7. Churn-freeze.

A very refreshing ice cream with a piquant taste of mint. The subtle flavor and rich bouquet of the herb teas add a distinctive taste to the custard base.

Use your favorite herb tea or try different combinations until you and your family decide on which blend you like best. All the herb teas respond well to spices and for a flavorful change add any of the following: cloves, cinnamon, cardamon, ginger, orange or lemon peel, nutmeg, or anise seed.

Some of the most common herb teas are:

Betony	—a relaxant, serve with a twist of orange peel
Camomile	—refreshing, soothing and tranquilizing
Ginger	—a stimulant to digestion
Linden	—a fine-flavored tea, wonderfully relaxing
Peppermint	—delicious and good for digestion
Verbena	—Exquisite flavor and smooth beverage
Yerba mate	—a stimulant and restorative tea

When preparing herb teas, always use a pottery or earthenware teapot, and make sure to bring your water to a rolling boil. If you like tea strong, use more herbs rather than increasing the brewing time. Herb teas should not be steeped more than 5 minutes. When using herb teabags, we noticed a great variance in the amount of weight of an individual teabag. Therefore, you may have to check individual brands and types for desired strength.

TIGER'S MILK® ICE CREAM

2 c. milk	2 egg yolks, slightly beaten
1½ T. arrowroot	¼ t. salt
½ c. honey	1 T. vanilla
½ c. Tiger's Milk, plain	2 c. heavy cream

1. Scald 1½ cups of the milk.
2. Mix arrowroot, honey, and Tiger's Milk together, and stir in the remaining ½ cup of cold milk.
3. Put arrowroot mixture in the top of a double boiler, slowly add the scalded milk, and cook, stirring constantly, for about 10 minutes.
4. Add slightly beaten egg yolks and cook 2 or 3 minutes longer.
5. Remove from the stove and cool quickly.
6. Add salt, vanilla, and heavy cream to the cooled mixture.
7. Churn-freeze.

Note: Tiger's Milk is a registered trademark of Plus Products, Irvine, California.

Delicious high-protein, nutritional custardy ice cream. Tiger's Milk Nutrition Booster is also available in flavors (natural vanilla, natural cocoa, and natural carob) for interesting, distinctive taste variations. Or a tablespoon of decaffeinated instant coffee may be added to the scalded milk for a coffee flavor. If added to carob, the coffee will produce a mocha flavor.

This would make a really delicious picker-upper breakfast quickie.

TOMATO ICE CREAM

3 c. chopped ripe tomatoes	pinch allspice
1 T. dried onion flakes	½ c. sesame seeds
¼ t. sea salt	1 c. heavy cream
pinch raw sugar	½ c. half and half
2 T. whole-wheat flour	2 egg whites
½ c. heavy cream	

1. Combine tomatoes, onion flakes, salt, and sugar in a small saucepan and simmer over low heat, stirring occasionally, for 10 minutes. Remove from heat and set aside.

2. Make a paste out of the flour and cream.

3. Put stewed tomatoes through a strainer and take the pulp out. Blend the pulp with the flour paste; add 1 cup of the tomato liquid and continue blending until smooth.

4. Add tomato mixture to the remaining ingredients, except for the egg whites.

5. Beat egg whites until stiff and fold into tomato mixture.

6. Churn-freeze.

Here is another gorgeous frozen soup to savor, sure to play a featured role at dinner parties. Start your meal with a few spoons of this tempting creamy pink delicacy.

With the year-around abundance of hothouse tomatoes, this could become a standard at all your parties. Once you become accustomed to the full flavor of a red ripe tomato, it will be hard to use those packaged products, which are picked before they are fully ripe so that they can survive shipping and handling.

After you develop a taste for frozen soups, you may enjoy this with some chopped fresh basil or dill or a garnish.

TOMATO YOGURT SHERBET

1 env. unflavored gelatin	1 T. lemon juice
2 T. cold water	3 T. finely chopped onions
3½ c. sliced tomatoes	1 t. celery seed
1 c. water	1 bay leaf
1 t. sea salt	1 c. yogurt
2 T. honey	

1. Dissolve gelatin in 2 tablespoons water for 5 minutes.

2. In a medium saucepan, combine all ingredients except the yogurt, and boil for 20 minutes. Remove from heat and press through a fine sieve or strainer. Cool the liquid.

3. Combine yogurt with the tomato liquid.

4. Churn-freeze.

This sherbet is similar to a tomato aspic, except that it has a richer, creamier consistency. It has a peppy, lively taste and is fine for summer luncheons. Serve on lettuce, surrounded by sliced cucumbers, fresh shrimp, or diced avocado.

The tomato, a fruit, has been eaten as a standard vegetable in our country since 1835. It is a tropical herb, closely related to the eggplant, pepper, and potato. There are so many varieties on the market that there are no "star" performers by name alone. Therefore, the wise shopper finds good tomatoes by judging their skin—smooth, glossy, and bright; the flesh is firm, but not hard. Misshapen, scarred tomatoes are really a poor buy, as the amount of waste makes them costly.

VANILLA Á LA BLENDER

½ c. raw sugar
1 t. arrowroot
pinch sea salt
2 egg yolks

1 T. vanilla
1 c. light cream
2 c. heavy cream

1. Place all ingredients except heavy cream in a blender and blend until smooth and creamy.
2. Combine mixture with heavy cream.
3. Churn-freeze.

Another of our marvelous "no cook" recipes. A tasty, satisfying, and creamy vanilla that can become the base for your favorite party desserts.

Vanilla Ice Cream Topping

To make an absolutely sensational ice cream sauce, take 1 pint of the ice cream, place in the refrigerator (not the freezing compartment) for 1 hour, or leave at room temperature for 15 minutes until soft. Whip 1 cup of heavy cream with an electric beater, remove from the bowl, and whip the softened ice cream until it is smooth. Fold the ice cream into the whipped cream and serve on your favorite warm pudding—especially apple brown betty. When preparing apple brown betty, think healthy and natural, and use one cup of honey and a half-cup of wheat germ for four tart cooking apples.

VANILLA ICE

3¼ c. water   1 2-in. piece vanilla bean,
½ c. raw sugar   split
                                  ¾ T. lemon juice

1. Mix together water, sugar, and vanilla bean. Place in top of a double boiler and boil for 10 minutes. Cool.
2. Strain mixture and add lemon juice.
3. Churn-freeze.

This is really a bare minimum but we wanted to include an ice that you can sweeten and flavor in any way you see fit. (1) Add 2 drops of cherry oil. (2) Add 1 cup of dry milk or soy milk and turn it into a sherbet. (3) Vary the flavoring as suggested in the recipe for Cottage Cheese Sherbet. Combination possibilities are endless.

Oranges á l'Orientale

If you want to celebrate a special event with a great dessert, try Oranges á l'Orientale. You won't believe what will happen to your plain vanilla ice.

Using a potato peeler, carefully remove peels from 6 oranges. Slice the peels toothpick thin and put in a saucepan, adding water to cover. Bring to a boil and drain. Repeat this procedure three times. Cover again with water, ½ cup of honey, and 1 vanilla bean. Simmer until slivers become crystal clear and liquid is syrupy. Remove any vanilla bean that may be left. Set aside and chill.

Peel all skin and membrane from oranges. Slice the oranges cross-wise; place around the inside edge of an attractive dessert glass, put a serving of vanilla ice in the center, and cover all over with the syrup and slivers.

VANILLA ICE CREAM
(French)

4 egg yolks	2 t. vanilla
¾ c. raw sugar	2 c. heavy cream
⅛ t. sea salt	1 c. half and half

1. Beat egg yolks until slightly thickened. Add sugar, salt, and vanilla.

2. Mix heavy cream and half and half together. Fold into egg mixture. Chill.

3. Churn-freeze.

Creamy, rich, and delightful. Vanilla is America's favorite (there are more than 200 flavors to choose from, yet almost half the ice cream eaten in our country is vanilla). The egg yolks create a firmer, better texture and a richer ice cream.

French Vanilla's distinguishing characteristic is egg yolks. However, recipes vary slightly in that (1) they use just yolks, as we did here; (2) they use whole eggs; or (3) they separate the egg, beat the yolk with the mix, and then fold in the white. You may want to experiment and discover just which one is your own personal favorite.

You can think of umpteen tasty additions for this classic recipe. For instance, for a coffee flavor dissolve 1½ tablespoons of instant decaffeinated coffee, or one of the coffee substitutes, in ¼ cup hot water, and add to the mix before freezing.

VANILLA ICE CREAM
(Natural Philadelphia)

3 c. light cream
10 T. raw sugar

1 vanilla bean (3-in. size, split)
pinch sea salt

1. Combine 1½ cups of the cream, sugar, vanilla bean, and salt in the top of a double boiler. Cook over low heat, stirring constantly, for 10 minutes. Remove beanpod; scrape pulp and *seeds* into the cream. Cool.
2. Add remaining 1½ cups of cream to the cooled mixture. Mix well.
3. Churn-freeze.

If you only try one ice cream in this entire book, or this is your first attempt at making ice cream, *this* is the recipe for you. You can be sure of good results and many compliments. When we think of how many different flavors there actually are, it's always a surprise to again discover how clean and wonderful plain vanilla tastes.

This is the true vanilla—light, elegant, and luscious. Traditionally, Philadelphia Vanilla is always made with vanilla bean. However, if not available, you can use 1 tablespoon of pure vanilla extract.

Biscuit Tortoni

Philadelphia Vanilla is so versatile it may well become your favorite mix. For a party dessert, try Biscuit Tortoni: When the ice cream comes out of the freezer can, reserve one pint, and keep it soft. In your blender place 4 macaroons, which you have crumbled, and some cut cherries (about 10) and ¼ cup slivered almonds. Blend finely. Fold the soft ice cream into the chopped ingredients. Spoon into 2- or 3-inch fluted paper cups; sprinkle with crumbled toasted almonds, pressing the crumbs lightly into the cream. Freeze until firm. This makes 4–5 servings.

For a bit of history: an Italian dessert fancier named Tortoni introduced this delicacy to the French at the end of the eighteenth century.

VANILLA ICE CREAM
(Sweet'n Sour)

1 c. plain yogurt	1½ c. milk
2 c. ricotta cheese	2 T. vanilla
½ c. honey	

1. Combine all ingredients until smooth and creamy.
2. Churn-freeze.

Tastes just like its name. An interesting base mix for yogurt fans; variations can be the same as those suggested for Cottage Cheese Ice Cream.

Be sure to get fresh ricotta cheese that has been continuously refrigerated or the flavor of the ice cream may be too tart. Ricotta cheese is made from fresh milk whey, after the curd has been removed for cheese making. About 10 percent milk or skim milk may have been added.

VANILLA SMOOTHIE
(Custard Ice Cream)

2 c. milk	2 egg yolks
1 T. arrowroot	pinch sea salt
¾ c. raw sugar	1 T. vanilla
½ c. nonfat dry milk powder	2 c. heavy cream

1. Scald 1½ cups of the milk in a small saucepan.

2. While the milk is being scalded, mix arrowroot, sugar, powdered milk, and the remaining ½ cup of milk together in the top of a double boiler. Make a smooth paste.

3. Slowly add the scalded milk to the mixture in the top of the double boiler and cook, stirring occasionally, for 10 minutes.

4. Beat the egg yolks with 2 tablespoons of the hot milk mixture; stirring slowly, add to the double boiler. Cook for an additional 5 minutes. Remove from heat. Cool.

5. While the mixture is cooling, stir it occasionally.

6. Add the rest of the ingredients.

7. Churn-freeze.

We wanted to give you a real custard base so that you can take off from there with any variation you choose. However, it's so satisfying that many people prefer to leave it as is; its lovely, smooth, full-bodied vanilla taste is exactly what they want. If you want to serve the ice cream right from the churn freezer without hardening, it will be just like the so-called soft ice cream sold commercially.

Carob Topping

For extra goodness, you'll especially like this dessert (and so will everyone else) served with a topping of carob syrup: Take 4 tablespoons carob powder, 2 tablespoons honey, 1 cup water, ¼ teaspoon vanilla, and 1 tablespoon butter; cook in a double boiler over moderate heat until thick and of syrup consistency. Even though carob tastes much like chocolate, it actually has a little more than half the calories, a hundredth the amount of fat, and two and one-half times the amount of calcium.

The Swirl

This ice cream would also make an excellent base for what is commonly known as vanilla fudge. While the ice cream is being churned, prepare the carob syrup and cool it. After you remove the ice cream from the dasher, take a large spoonful of the syrup, put it on top of the ice cream, and with your spoon push it down in a swirling motion so that it is rippled throughout. Other syrups made from your favorite fruits can also be used to produce this ripple for different flavorings.

WATERMELON SHERBET

3 t. agar flakes
3 c. watermelon purée
½ c. honey
¼ t. cinnamon

½ t. lemon juice
1 T. grated lemon rind
pinch sea salt
1 c. milk

1. Soften agar flakes in ¼ cup of the watermelon purée. Mix gently and heat in a double boiler for a few minutes to dissolve the agar flakes. Cool.
2. Add remaining watermelon purée and other ingredients. Mix well.
3. Churn-freeze.

Horray! Watermelon without pits and squirting juice! Just a refreshing, thirst-quenching dainty dessert with a delicate sweet flavor. Top with a small sprig of fresh mint. For those of you who don't use animal protein we've made this recipe with agar flakes (the sea vegetable that many people use for thickening) to show that it stabilizes just as well as gelatin in frozen desserts.

The surest guide to a watermelon's ripeness is taste. However, if you wish, thump it—a ripe melon chimes a deep hollow note. Also, it should be symetrically shaped and firm, with a somewhat velvety (not shiny) bloom on the rind. If you buy a melon that's been cut, you'll have a much easier time since the important consideration is firm red flesh and black or dark-brown seeds. Store melons away from sunlight and at a temperature of 70°. They will keep in the refrigerator for up to a week.

This melon is a good source of important minerals (calcium, magnesium, phosphorous, and potassium), and a 1½ inch slice usually provides about 50 percent of the adult daily requirements of vitamins A and C. It also contains thiamine (vitamin B). All this nutritional information may come as quite a surprise to those people who thought watermelon was just refreshing sweet water.

YOGURT SHERBET

2 c. yogurt
1 c. milk
1¼ c. honey

1 c. grape juice
¼ c. lemon juice
2 eggs

1. Combine yogurt, milk, honey, grape juice, and lemon juice; blend until smooth and creamy.
2. Beat eggs until light and fluffy and fold into yogurt mixture.
3. Churn-freeze.

A light, fluffy sherbet to gratify yogurt fans. The freshest, purest, sweetest, and best-tasting yogurt is that which you make yourself and your sherbet will reflect it. If you haven't done so as yet, try making yogurt as we suggested following the Orange Yogurt Crunch recipe. Put your creative ability to the test; anything you do with this sherbet will please you.

Rose Hips Yogurt Sherbet

To prove its versatility, we went wild with this one. In one of our visits to a local natural foods shop, we found a special group of purées that we thought would be just right for any of our base recipes. Rose hips intrigued us; we tasted it and found it similar to apricot; after combining with honey and freezing, the strong taste of the purée lessened, and it proved to be a pleasing dessert. Use one cup of the rose hips purée; you'll be happy with the results. Rose hips, the fruit of the rose that remains after the petals have fallen off, are so rich in vitamin C that everyone should use them. During World War II, the English extracted quantities of vitamin C from rose hips. If you're not familiar with it, we hope this will be your introduction.

Kumquat Topping

Another original is a kumquat topping. This small orangelike fruit usually available in abundance from November to February is edible in its entirety. The rind is sweet, the juice is tart.

Slice a pound of kumquats into small pieces. Mix 1 tablespoon arrowroot with ¾ cup honey, a pinch of sea salt, ⅛ teaspoon cinnamon, a pinch of ground cloves, and 1 tablespoon lemon juice. Combine the kumquats with the other ingredients and simmer in a saucepan for 10 minutes.

Cool and spoon over the sherbet.

ZUCCHINI JULIA

2 c. zucchini purée	½ t. ginger
½ c. raw sugar	½ t. nutmeg
pinch sea salt	¼ t. mace
2 eggs	½ c. half and half
1 t. cinnamon	1 c. heavy cream

1. Place all ingredients in an electric blender and blend until smooth and creamy. Chill.
2. Churn-freeze.

This dessert was created as the result of a wishful lament by *chef extraordinaire* Julia Child for a zucchini ice cream, and we think we've come up with a winner in this speckled green, impressive, and delicious dessert. Those of you who remember the old-fashioned squash pie will certainly welcome this satisfying dessert, which is particularly delicate and light tasting.

Zucchini (also called Italian squash) is one of the many varieties of summer squash. It has a tender thin green skin and may be cooked without paring, as the skin is edible.

ZESTY ZUCCHINI SPECIAL

2 c. zucchini slices	½ c. light cream
½ c. chicken broth	pinch sea salt
2 T. dried onion flakes	2 T. dried orange peel
1 c. cottage cheese	½ c. honey
1 c. sour cream	⅓ c. lemon juice
⅓ c. orange juice	

1. In a small saucepan, place zucchini, chicken broth, and onion flakes and cook until tender. Cool.

2. Place in blender with all the other ingredients; blend until smooth and creamy.

3. Churn-freeze.

A most unusual blend—a natural complement to your favorite combination of salad greens. Would also be superb if served as a piquant relish with chicken, turkey, or veal.

When cooking zucchini, remember that it should always be steamed rapidly.

Zucchini by itself has a very delicate taste that had to be emphasized before freezing. That is why we used so many different ingredients in this recipe. Once you try it, we think you will introduce a new element into many of your favorite meals.

Glossary of Terms

BEAT— Mix with a strong constant motion using a spoon, rotary beater, electric mixer, or blender until smooth.

BLEND— Stir gently two or more ingredients until completely combined. This term may also mean to mix in a blender, in which case don't overdo.

CHILL— Place in a refrigerator or another cool atmosphere until mixture is cool throughout. For quick chilling, place the pot containing the warm mixture in a pan with cold or ice water. If you stir, it will be at the ready point soon.

COOL— Not as cold as chill. If there is time, you can let the mixture stand at room temperature in a cool place until lukewarm.

COOK, STIRRING CONSTANTLY— Stir gently and steadily with a spoon so that mixture thickens evenly.

CRUSH— Mash in mortar, with rolling pin or some other utensil, until food is granular or powdered.

DICE— Cut into small (about ⅛-inch) cubes.

DISSOLVE— Stir a dry or solid substance into a liquid solution.

FOLD— Really means fold in gently without loosing the bubbles. Generally, beaten eggs, egg whites alone, and or whipped creams are placed on top of another mixture, then combined with a slow easy motion. A favorite way is to cut through the center with a spatula or spoon. sweep the bottom, bring some mixture up the side, and dump it on top with a continuous motion.

GRATE— Rub on a grater to produce fine pieces. These may be particle size when used to enhance the taste.

PARE— Cut off the outer covering (skin) with a sharp knife.

PEEL— This differs from pare in that the skin can usually be pulled off with the fingers.

PURÉE— Reduce to consistency of mush by forcing through a food mill or fine sieve or placing in a blender for a few moments. The blender may have to be stopped and the food pushed back into the path of the cutters if it does not fall back by itself.

SCALD— Heat liquid (generally in a double-boiler top) to just below the boiling point. At the right heat, tiny bubbles appear around the edge.

SIMMER— This is usually for a longer time than scalding and should be done at a lower heat. An occasional small bubble is all right but lower the heat if many appear.

STIR— Mix gently with a spoon, using a one-direction circular motion. In the process, scrape the sides and bottom of the bowl.

WHIP— Much more vigorous than stir. Beat rapidly to incorporate air. The volume will naturally increase. This can be done with a spoon, wire whisk, rotary beater, electric mixer, or blender.

Equivalent Weights and Measures

t.: teaspoon
T.: tablespoon
c.: cup

Dash (liquid): a few drops
Pinch (dry, the amount that can be held between the tip
  of index finger and the thumb): slightly less than ⅛ t.

3 t.	1 T.	½ fl. oz.
1½ t.	½ T.	
2 T.	⅛ c.	1 fl. oz.
4 T.	¼ c.	2 fl. oz.
5 T. plus 1 t.	⅓ c.	
8 T.	½ c.	4 fl. oz.
10 T. plus 2 t.	⅔ c.	
12 T.	¾ c.	6 fl. oz.
16 T.	1 c.	8 fl. oz.
2 c.	1 pt.	16 fl. oz.
4 c.	1 qt.	32 fl. oz.
1 gal.	4 qt. (liquid)	
1 peck	8 qt. (dry)	

Equivalent Food Amounts

Food	Weight or Number	Measure
Apples	1 lb. (3 medium)	3 c., sliced
Bananas	1 lb. (3 medium)	2½ c., sliced
Berries	1 qt.	3½ c.
Butter	¼ lb.	½ c.
Cottage cheese	½ lb. (8 oz.)	1 c.
Cream cheese	8 oz.	1 c.
Dates	6¼ oz.	1 c.
Eggs	5 large	1 c.
Egg whites	8–10	1 c.
Egg yolks	12–15	1 c.
Figs	5–13 oz.	1 c.
Flour	1 lb.	4 c.
Gelatin	¼ oz. envelope	1 T.
Heavy cream	½ pt.	2 c., after whipping
Honey	1 t.	¼ oz.
Lemon	1 medium lemon	¼ c. juice
Lemon rind, grated	1 medium lemon	1 T.
Nuts, chopped	5 oz.	1 c.
Orange	1 medium orange	⅓–½ c. juice
Orange rind, grated	1 medium orange	2 T.
Prunes or apricots	½ lb.	1¼ c.
Raisins	5 oz.	1 c.
Sugar (raw)	1 lb.	2¼ c.
Tangerine	6 medium tangerines	1 c. juice

Substitutes

Instead of	Use
1 T. arrowroot	2 T. flour
1 c. buttermilk	1 T. lemon juice or vinegar plus enough sweet milk to make 1 c. (let stand 5 minutes)
1 T. cornstarch	1 T. arrowroot
1 T. flour	½ T. arrowroot
2 egg yolks	1 whole egg
1 T. gelatin	3 t. agar flakes
1 c. honey	¾ c. sugar plus ¼ c. liquid
1 c. fresh milk	⅓ c. instant nonfat dry milk plus 1 c. water
1 c. sour cream	1 c. yogurt or buttermilk or 3 T. butter plus ⅞ c. sour milk
1 c. granulated sugar	¾ c. honey and reduce liquid in recipe by ¼ c. or 1 c. sorghum or ¾ c. unsulfured and ¼ c. blackstrap molasses or 1 c. unsulfured molasses or 1¼ or 1½ c. maple syrup, carob syrup, or malt syrup (Taste will vary accordingly.)
1 square chocolate	3 T. carob powder plus 2 T. water
1 T. vanilla extract	1 3-in. piece vanilla bean

Index

153

Self help & reference